FLAVOUR FRESH
VEGETARIAN
recipes

CONTENTS

EDITORIAL
Food Editor Sheryle Eastwood
Assistant Food Editor Rachel Blackmore
Home Economist Anneka Mitchell
Recipe Development Jane Ash, Penny Cox,
Sue Geraghty, Meg Thorley
Food Consultant Frances Naldrett
Nutrition Consultant Helen O'Connor
Text Denise Greig, Alison Magney
Editorial Co-ordinator Margaret Kelly
Subeditor Ella Martin

PHOTOGRAPHY
Yanto Noriento

STYLING
Wendy Berecry
Marie Hélène Clauzon

ILLUSTRATIONS
Jill MacLeod

PRODUCTION
Tracy Burt, Margie Mulray, Chris Hatcher

COVER DESIGN
Frank Pithers

DESIGN AND PRODUCTION MANAGER
Nadia Sbisa

PUBLISHER
Philippa Sandall

Published by J.B. Fairfax Press Pty Ltd
80-82 McLachlan Avenue
Rushcutters Bay 2011

Includes Index
ISBN 1 86343 014 8

Formatted by J.B. Fairfax Press Pty Ltd
Output by Adtype, Sydney
Printed by Toppan Printing Co, Hong Kong

Distributed in Australia by
Newsagents Direct Distributors
150 Bourke Road, Alexandria NSW

Distributed Internationally by
T.B. Clarke (Overseas) Pty Ltd
80 McLachlan Avenue
Rushcutters Bay NSW 2011
Tel: (02) 360 7566
Fax: (02) 360 7445

Distributed in UK by
J.B. Fairfax Press Ltd
9 Trinity Centre, Park Farm Estate
Wellingborough, Northants
Ph: (0933) 402330 Fax: (0933) 402234

New Zealand agents
Medialine Holdings Ltd
P O Box 100 243
North Shore Mail Centre
Tel: (09) 443 0250 Fax: (09) 443 0249

METRIC MEASURES

1.25 mL	$^1/_4$ teaspoon
2.5 mL	$^1/_2$ teaspoon
5 mL	1 teaspoon
20 mL	1 tablespoon
60 mL	$^1/_4$ cup
80 mL	$^1/_3$ cup
125 mL	$^1/_2$ cup
250 mL	1 cup

CHECK-AND-GO

When planning a meal, use the easy Check-and-Go boxes which appear beside each ingredient. Simply check on your pantry shelf and if the ingredients are not there, tick the boxes as a reminder to add those items to your shopping list.

FOOD
for thought

Fresh, light, delicious – these are not words that many people associate with vegetarianism. That is, until now. Vegetarianism has, for far too long, been associated in people's minds with 'gluggy' bowls of brown rice, plates of boiled lentils, indigestible slabs of 'good-for-you' pies which, rather than being feather light and delectable, sit on your stomach for hours. Banish those ideas forever.

The influence of Asian cooking styles, such as stir-frying and steaming, have been eagerly embraced by imaginative vegetarian cooks, with the result that vibrantly coloured vegetables, stir-fried in a trice, sprinkled with fresh coriander leaves and accompanied by a little steamed Basmati rice are winning over traditional meat eaters.

Today, people are increasingly turning to delicious, inexpensive and healthy vegetarian fare as an alternative to the traditional meaty mains. Whether you want occasional meatless meals or a completely vegetarian diet, you will find many imaginative suggestions in this beautifully photographed book.

More than ever before, people want to experience their natural energy, and to simply feel 'good'. Light, meatless eating is one widely acknowledged way to achieve this goal.

Vegetarian diets are usually lower in fat and higher in fibre than diets which include meat. Seventh Day Adventists, who eat a varied vegetarian diet, have a good health record. They are less likely to be overweight and they have fewer people with heart disease, high blood pressure and cancer compared with the rest of the population. However, it must also be remembered that they lead a generally healthy lifestyle and neither smoke nor drink alcohol.

Well-balanced vegetarian diets are now known to be nutritionally adequate, especially those that include milk and eggs. Very severe diets can be a problem, although with careful planning these too can be nutritionally sound. Strict macrobiotic or fruitarian diets (fruit only) cannot provide all the nutrients you need for good health.

When planning a vegetarian diet, you must be careful to include the nutrients you need for good health. This is especially important for children and for pregnant women and breastfeeding mothers, who have greater nutritional needs. Because of the bulky nature of the vegetarian diet, children sometimes cannot eat enough energy and protein. However, this is less likely to be a problem in diets which include milk and eggs.

Vegetarianism suffered from a reputation of seriousness, in the bad old days, but now, innovation and fun are the key words. You'll be astounded at the variety of cooking styles and ingredients that this book introduces, and the bold, different ways in which these ingredients have been put together.

If you are 'new' to vegetarianism, look at our chapters on Vegetarian Foods Explained, Vegetarian Essentials and Easy Menu Planning for advice and inspiration.

If you are not new to vegetarianism, a quick look through our recipes might well take you back to the culinary drawing board!

Welcome to the new vegetarianism – you have nothing to lose but your old prejudices.

In recent years there has been a renewed interest in vegetarianism. Although cultural and religious groups have practised vegetarianism for centuries, an increasing number of people are now adopting a vegetarian diet for a variety of reasons: philosophical, economical, religious, humanitarian, health or ecological.

Given that 'meat on the plate' has traditionally been a sign of aristocracy or wealth, it is interesting to find that the vegetarian diet is now an acceptable, even fashionable, alternative. This attitude is far from the traditional view of vegetarians who were often labelled as eccentrics or lunatics!

If you want to eat a vegetarian diet, variety and balance are the keys to success, as for all diets. If you are just adopting a vegetarian diet, it is a good idea to modify your eating habits gradually as you become more familiar with the diet. Since the vegetarian diet is high in complex carbohydrate and fibre, low in fat and refined sugars, it embraces many of the dietary guidelines for good health. Given this and the increased social acceptance of vegetarianism, perhaps more people will experiment with vegetarian-style meals, or at least increased amounts of vegetables and fruits in their diet.

DO YOU KNOW?

Which of the following were vegetarian?

- ☐ Pythagoras
- ☐ William Shakespeare
- ☐ Aristotle
- ☐ Charles Dickens
- ☐ John Milton
- ☐ George Bernard Shaw

Answer: Pythagoras, Aristotle, John Milton, George Bernard Shaw

A little taste of something delicious is good for the soul, not to mention children's morning break at school, mid-afternoon in a frantic office, or whenever time is short and food is needed.

TASTY TOPPERS
and fancy fillers

❖

FRUITY BANANA AND CAMEMBERT MUFFINS

This combination of fruit and cheese is sure to be a popular snack no matter what time of the day.

Serves 4

- ☐ **1 large banana, peeled and sliced**
- ☐ **$^1/_2$ green apple, chopped**
- ☐ **$^1/_2$ stalk celery, sliced**
- ☐ **3 tablespoons chopped pecan nuts**
- ☐ **2 teaspoons desiccated coconut**
- ☐ **2 tablespoons mayonnaise**
- ☐ **4 fruit muffins, halved and buttered**
- ☐ **125 g (4 oz) Camembert cheese, sliced**

Combine banana, apple, celery, pecans, coconut and mayonnaise. Spoon onto muffin halves and top with Camembert slices. Grill under a medium heat until cheese melts. Serve immediately.

❖

CHILLI BEAN TACOS

Tacos are always a welcome light meal or snack, and these delicious bean-filled ones take next to no time to prepare.

Serves 4

- ☐ **440 g (14 oz) canned red kidney beans, drained and rinsed**
- ☐ **1 teaspoon ground cumin**
- ☐ **1 tomato, peeled and chopped**
- ☐ **1 teaspoon chilli sauce**
- ☐ **8 taco shells**
- ☐ **4 lettuce leaves, shredded**
- ☐ **grated tasty cheese**

1   Place kidney beans, cumin, tomato and chilli sauce in a saucepan and cook over a medium heat for 3-4 minutes or until heated through.
2   Arrange taco shells on an oven tray and heat at 180°C (350°F/Gas 4) for 5 minutes or until heated through. Fill taco shells with bean mixture. Top with shredded lettuce and cheese. Serve immediately.

❖

FRENCH ONION ROLLS

Serves 4

- ☐ **4 wholemeal rolls**
- ☐ **15 g ($^1/_2$ oz) polyunsaturated margarine**
- ☐ **1 large onion, sliced**
- ☐ **2 eggs, lightly beaten**
- ☐ **125 g (4 oz) thick sour cream**
- ☐ **3 tablespoons evaporated skim milk**
- ☐ **$^1/_2$ teaspoon ground nutmeg**
- ☐ **1 teaspoon horseradish cream**
- ☐ **freshly ground black pepper**
- ☐ **125 g (4 oz) grated tasty cheese**

1   Scoop out centre of rolls, leaving about 1 cm ($^1/_2$ in) thick shell. Place rolls on an oven tray and set aside.
2   Melt margarine in a frypan and cook onion for 4-5 minutes or until golden. Divide onion between rolls.
3   Place eggs, sour cream, skim milk, nutmeg, and horseradish cream in a bowl. Mix to combine and season to taste with pepper. Spoon egg mixture into rolls, top with cheese and bake at 200°C (400°F/ Gas 6) for 20-25 minutes or until firm.

Fruity Banana and Camembert Muffins, Chilli Bean Tacos, French Onion Rolls

DEVILLED SOUFFLE MUSHROOM CAPS

Serves 4

- [ ] **8 large flat mushroom caps**
- [ ] **30 g (1 oz) polyunsaturated margarine, melted**

DEVILLED FILLING
- [ ] **15 g (^{1}/2 oz) polyunsaturated margarine**
- [ ] **4 tablespoons slivered almonds**
- [ ] **1 green pepper, finely chopped**
- [ ] **1^1/2 teaspoons curry powder**
- [ ] **1^1/2 teaspoons dry mustard**
- [ ] **2 teaspoons brown sugar**
- [ ] **2 tablespoons tomato sauce**
- [ ] **1 teaspoon Worcestershire sauce**

SOUFFLE TOPPING
- [ ] **2 egg whites**
- [ ] **1 tablespoon mayonnaise**
- [ ] **4 tablespoons grated tasty cheese**

1   Remove stems from mushrooms, chop finely and set aside. Wipe mushroom caps with a damp cloth. Brush mushroom caps with margarine and place on an oven tray.

2   To make filling, melt margarine in a frypan and cook almonds for 1-2 minutes or until just golden. Add pepper and mushroom stems and stir-fry for 2 minutes. Stir in curry powder, mustard and brown sugar, cook for 1 minute. Combine tomato and Worcestershire sauces and add to pan. Cook until just heated through, then remove pan from heat. Divide filling between mushroom caps.

3   To make souffle topping, beat egg whites until stiff peaks form. Fold through mayonnaise and spoon mixture over mushrooms. Top with cheese and bake at 220°C (425°F/Gas 7) for 8-10 minutes, or until topping is well puffed and golden.

❖

CURRIED LETTUCE ROLLS

Serves 4

- [ ] **30 g (1 oz) polyunsaturated margarine**
- [ ] **3 teaspoons curry powder**
- [ ] **1 onion, chopped**
- [ ] **2 stalks celery, chopped**
- [ ] **2 large ripe tomatoes, peeled and chopped**
- [ ] **1 red pepper, seeded and chopped**
- [ ] **440 g (14 oz) canned red kidney beans, drained and rinsed**
- [ ] **freshly ground black pepper**
- [ ] **8 large iceberg lettuce leaves, blanched**

DRESSING
- [ ] **1 tablespoon olive oil**
- [ ] **3 tablespoons red wine vinegar**
- [ ] **1 tablespoon concentrated tomato paste**
- [ ] **1 tablespoon chopped fresh coriander**
- [ ] **^{1}/4 teaspoon ground cumin**
- [ ] **freshly ground black pepper**

1   Melt margarine in a saucepan and cook curry powder, onion and celery for 3 minutes. Stir in tomatoes, pepper and kidney beans. Cover and simmer for 15 minutes or until thick. Season to taste with pepper. Spoon bean mixture onto lettuce leaves and roll up firmly to secure.

2   To make dressing, place oil, vinegar, tomato paste, coriander and cumin in a screw-top jar and shake well to combine. Season to taste with pepper. To serve, drizzle dressing over rolls.

Devilled Souffle Mushroom Caps, Curried Lettuce Rolls

Plates Les Olivades

Tomato and Mozzarella Pizza Subs, Pitta Pizza Roll-Ups, Nachos

❖❖

TOMATO AND MOZZARELLA PIZZA SUBS

Ideal for after-school fare.

Serves 2

- ☐ **2 long wholemeal rolls, split and toasted**
- ☐ **2 tablespoons concentrated tomato paste**
- ☐ **1 small onion, finely sliced**
- ☐ **1 tablespoon finely chopped fresh basil**
- ☐ **4 olives, pitted and sliced**
- ☐ **1 tablespoon pine nuts**
- ☐ **30 g (1 oz) mozzarella cheese, grated**
- ☐ **freshly ground black pepper**

1 Spread each half roll with tomato paste. Top with onion, then sprinkle with basil, olives, pine nuts and cheese. Season to taste with pepper.

2 Grill under a medium heat for 4-5 minutes, or until cheese melts.

❖

NACHOS

Serves 4

- ☐ **155 g (5 oz) corn chips**
- ☐ **2 tomatoes, peeled and finely chopped**
- ☐ **125 g (4 oz) grated mozzarella cheese**
- ☐ **125 g (4 oz) grated tasty cheese**

AVOCADO TOPPING
- ☐ **2 small avocados, stoned, peeled and chopped**
- ☐ **2 teaspoons lemon juice**
- ☐ **1 small onion, grated**
- ☐ **2 cloves garlic, crushed**
- ☐ **1 teaspoon chilli sauce**

1 Layer corn chips, tomatoes and cheese in an ovenproof dish, finishing with a layer of cheese. Bake at 200°C (400°F/Gas 6) for 10-15 minutes, or until cheese melts and is golden.

2 To make topping, place avocados, lemon juice, onion, garlic and chilli sauce in a food processor or blender and process until smooth. Spoon onto corn chips and serve immediately.

❖

PITTA PIZZA ROLL-UPS

Serves 6

- ☐ **3 tablespoons concentrated tomato paste**
- ☐ **2 tablespoons chopped fresh basil**
- ☐ **3 tablespoons chopped pitted black olives**
- ☐ **6 large pitta bread rounds**
- ☐ **200 g (6¹/₂ oz) mushrooms, finely chopped**
- ☐ **1 small red pepper, finely sliced**
- ☐ **1 onion, chopped**
- ☐ **200 g (6¹/₂ oz) ricotta cheese**
- ☐ **200 g (6¹/₂ oz) grated mozzarella cheese**

1 Combine tomato paste, basil and olives. Divide mixture into six portions and spread over pitta bread. Top with mushrooms, pepper, onion and ricotta cheese. Press down lightly, then roll up tightly and secure with a toothpick.

2 Place rolls on an oven tray and sprinkle with mozzarella cheese. Bake at 220°C (425°F/Gas 7) for 15-20 minutes, or until heated through and cheese melts.

❖

SPINACH SLAW

Serves 4

- ☐ **250 g (8 oz) finely shredded spinach leaves**
- ☐ **1 carrot, grated**
- ☐ **100 g (3¹/₂ oz) sultanas**
- ☐ **100 g (3¹/₂ oz) roasted peanuts, chopped**
- ☐ **125 g (4 oz) mayonnaise**
- ☐ **freshly ground black pepper**

Combine spinach, carrot, sultanas, peanuts and mayonnaise. Season to taste with pepper and use as desired.

❖

CARAWAY SLAW TOPPING

Serves 4

- ☐ **100 g (3¹/₂ oz) cabbage, finely shredded**
- ☐ **2 teaspoons caraway seeds**
- ☐ **2 teaspoons wholegrain mustard**
- ☐ **1 tablespoon mayonnaise**
- ☐ **8 slices Swiss cheese**
- ☐ **4 dill pickles, sliced lengthways**

Combine cabbage, caraway seeds, mustard and mayonnaise. Divide between four slices of bread, then top each slice with 2 slices of cheese and 2 slices of dill pickles.

❖

COOL CUCUMBER TOPPING

Serves 4

- ☐ **1 telegraph cucumber, diced**
- ☐ **125 g (4 oz) unflavoured yogurt**
- ☐ **1 tablespoon finely chopped fresh dill**

Combine cucumber, yogurt and dill and use as desired.

❖

GORGONZOLA AND WALNUTS

Serves 4

- ☐ **200 g (6¹/₂ oz) Gorgonzola cheese, mashed**
- ☐ **125 g (4 oz) walnuts, chopped**
- ☐ **8 cos lettuce leaves**
- ☐ **30 g (1 oz) alfalfa sprouts**

Combine Gorgonzola cheese and walnuts. Line pitta pockets, or top bread slices, with lettuce leaves, then top with Gorgonzola mixture and alfalfa sprouts.

❖

CHEESE ASPARAGUS TOPPING

Serves 4

- ☐ **315 g (10 oz) canned asparagus tips, drained**
- ☐ **1 teaspoon wholegrain mustard**
- ☐ **1 tablespoon mayonnaise**
- ☐ **60 g (2 oz) Gorgonzola cheese, crumbled**

Place asparagus, mustard and mayonnaise in a small bowl and mash to combine. Spread over four slices of bread and sprinkle with cheese.

Variation

You might like to place this topping on toasted bread, then grill and serve hot.

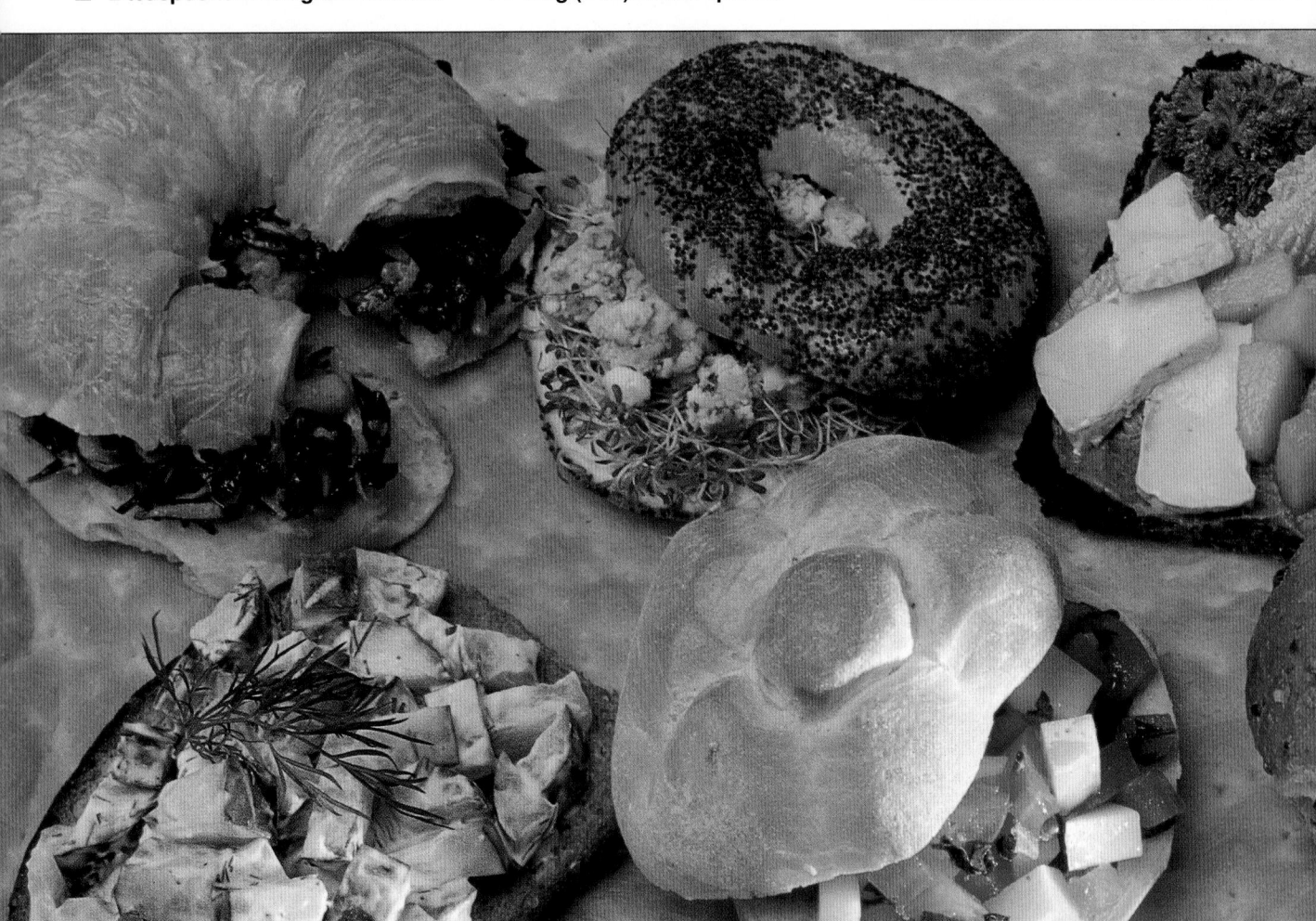

GARDEN FRESH VEGETABLE AND SALAD PLATTER

This platter is ideal to serve as a light meal, snack or starter for a barbecue.

Serves 4

- ☐ 4 slices processed, tasty cheese
- ☐ 1 large tomato, cut into sixths
- ☐ 1 small cucumber, cut into thin strips
- ☐ 8 canned asparagus spears
- ☐ 8 radishes
- ☐ 2 hard-boiled eggs, sliced
- ☐ 155 g (5 oz) button mushrooms, sliced
- ☐ 1 large stalk celery, cut into thin strips

DILL DIPPING SAUCE
- ☐ 2 tablespoons mayonnaise
- ☐ 4 tablespoons unflavoured yogurt
- ☐ 1 teaspoon grated lemon rind
- ☐ 2 tablespoons finely chopped fresh dill

1 Arrange cheese slices, tomato, cucumber, asparagus, radishes, eggs, mushrooms and celery attractively on a platter.
2 To make sauce, combine mayonnaise, yogurt, lemon rind and dill in a bowl. Mix well to combine and serve with vegetable and salad platter.

ROCKMELON CAMEMBERT TOPPING

Serves 4

- ☐ French mustard
- ☐ rocket leaves
- ☐ 125 g (4 oz) Camembert cheese, sliced
- ☐ 1/2 small rockmelon, peeled, seeded and diced

1 Spread each slice of bread with French mustard to taste.
2 Top with rocket leaves, Camembert cheese and rockmelon.

MEXICAN PUMPKIN SEED DIP

You might like to serve this dip on a vegetable platter in place of (or as well as) the Dill Dipping Sauce.

Serves 6

- ☐ 100 g (3 1/2 oz) Mexican pumpkin seeds, toasted
- ☐ 1 tablespoon lemon juice
- ☐ 2 tablespoons balsamic vinegar
- ☐ 1 clove garlic, crushed
- ☐ 1/2 teaspoon Dijon-style mustard

Place pumpkin seeds, lemon juice, vinegar, garlic and mustard in a food processor or blender and process until smooth. Chill before serving.

TOMATOES AND MOZZARELLA

Serves 4

- ☐ 4 tomatoes, chopped
- ☐ 125 g (4 oz) mozzarella cheese, cubed
- ☐ 2 tablespoons finely chopped fresh basil
- ☐ 100 g (3 1/2 oz) pitted black olives
- ☐ 2 tablespoons cider vinegar
- ☐ 1 tablespoon olive oil
- ☐ freshly ground black pepper

Combine tomatoes, cheese, basil and olives. Mix together vinegar and oil, pour over tomato mixture and toss to combine. Season to taste with black pepper and use as desired.

From left: Toppers and fillings on a selection of bread: Spinach Slaw, Gorgonzola and Walnuts, Rockmelon Camembert Topping, Cheese Asparagus Topping, Caraway Slaw Topping, Tomatoes and Mozzarella, Cool Cucumber Topping; Garden Fresh Vegetable and Salad Platter, Mexican Pumpkin Seed Dip

A tasty soup or starter can really tantalise your tastebuds. This chapter shows you how to make mouthwatering starters and sides for all occasions.

SUPER STARTERS
and sensational sides

❖
SPINACH AND TOMATO CREPE BAKE

Serves 6

- [ ] **4 tablespoons wholemeal plain flour, sifted and grits returned**
- [ ] **4 tablespoons buckwheat flour, sifted**
- [ ] **1 egg, lightly beaten**
- [ ] **250 mL (8 fl oz) milk**
- [ ] **1 tablespoon vegetable oil**

FILLING
- [ ] **500 g (1 lb) spinach washed, stalks removed and leaves chopped**
- [ ] **15 g (^{1}/2 oz) polyunsaturated margarine**
- [ ] **1 onion, finely chopped**
- [ ] **375 g (12 oz) ricotta cheese**
- [ ] **1 tablespoon grated Parmesan cheese**
- [ ] **^{1}/2 teaspoon ground (grated) nutmeg**
- [ ] **60 g (2 oz) pine nuts, toasted**
- [ ] **freshly ground black pepper**
- [ ] **90 g (3 oz) grated tasty cheese**

TOMATO SAUCE
- [ ] **125 mL) (4 fl oz) vegetable stock**
- [ ] **440 g (14 oz) canned tomatoes, undrained and mashed**
- [ ] **1 tablespoon concentrated tomato paste**
- [ ] **^{1}/2 teaspoon sugar**
- [ ] **1 tablespoon finely chopped fresh basil**

1 Combine wholemeal and buckwheat flours in a bowl. Whisk together egg, milk and oil. Gradually add to flour mixture and mix to a smooth batter. Cover and set aside for 30 minutes. Pour 2-3 tablespoons of batter into a greased and heated, small heavy-based frypan and cook until lightly browned on each side. Repeat with remaining batter.

2 To make filling, boil, steam or microwave spinach until tender. Drain well and set aside. Melt margarine in a saucepan and cook onion for 5 minutes or until softened. Place spinach, onion, ricotta cheese, Parmesan cheese, nutmeg and pine nuts in a bowl. Mix to combine. Season to taste with pepper.

3 Spoon spinach mixture into centre of crepes and roll up. Place in a lightly oiled ovenproof dish and sprinkle with cheese. Bake at 180°C (350°F/Gas 4) for 25 minutes, or until heated through.

4 To make sauce, place stock, tomatoes, tomato paste, sugar and basil in a saucepan and cook for 5 minutes or until sauce thickens. Spoon over crepes and serve.

❖
MINTED PEA AND WATERCRESS SOUP

Serves 4

- [ ] **30 g (1 oz) margarine**
- [ ] **1 onion, finely chopped**
- [ ] **1 clove garlic, crushed**
- [ ] **1 bunch watercress, chopped**
- [ ] **250 g (8 oz) frozen green peas**
- [ ] **750 mL (1^1/4 pt) vegetable stock**
- [ ] **freshly ground black pepper**
- [ ] **2 tablespoons finely chopped fresh mint**
- [ ] **4 tablespoons unflavoured yogurt**

1 Melt margarine in a large saucepan and cook onion and garlic for 3-4 minutes, or until onion softens. Stir in watercress, peas and stock. Bring to the boil, reduce heat, cover and simmer for 15 minutes. Season to taste with pepper.

2 Transfer soup to a food processor or blender and process until smooth. Return to a clean saucepan, stir in mint and heat for 2-3 minutes. Serve hot, or chilled, in individual bowls with a swirl of yogurt.

❖
THAI VEGETABLE PUFFS WITH DIPPING SAUCE

Spice-laden, savoury-filled parcels served with a traditional Thai dipping sauce.

Makes 24

- [ ] **375 g (12 oz) prepared or ready-rolled puff pastry, thawed**
- [ ] **vegetable oil for cooking**

FILLING
- [ ] **30 g (1 oz) polyunsaturated margarine**
- [ ] **1 teaspoon curry powder**
- [ ] **^{1}/2 teaspoon ground cumin**
- [ ] **^{1}/2 teaspoon garam masala**
- [ ] **1 small onion, finely chopped**
- [ ] **1 large carrot, grated**
- [ ] **1 zucchini (courgette), grated**
- [ ] **1 tablespoon crunchy peanut butter**
- [ ] **2 large potatoes, cooked and mashed**

DIPPING SAUCE
- [ ] **250 mL (8 fl oz) white vinegar**
- [ ] **185 g (6 oz) white sugar**
- [ ] **1 small red chilli, finely chopped**
- [ ] **1 small cucumber, peeled, seeded and finely chopped**

1 Roll out pastry to 3 mm (^{1}/8 in) thickness. Using a 7.5 cm (3 in) round pastry cutter, cut 24 pastry rounds.

2 To make filling, melt margarine in a saucepan, stir in curry powder, cumin and garam masala and cook for 1 minute. Add onion, carrot and zucchini (courgette), and cook until vegetables are tender. Stir in peanut butter and combine with potatoes.

3 Lay a pastry round in the palm of your hand and place a teaspoon of filling in the centre. Wet edge of the pastry with a little water, fold pastry over filling and pinch edges together. Repeat with remaining pastry rounds and filling.

4 To make sauce, place vinegar and sugar in a small saucepan and cook over low heat, stirring frequently, without boiling, until sugar dissolves. Mix in chilli and cucumber, bring to the boil, then reduce heat and simmer uncovered for 5 minutes or until sauce thickens slightly.

5 Heat oil in a large saucepan and cook puffs for 3-4 minutes or until crisp and golden. Drain on absorbent kitchen paper and serve with dipping sauce.

Thai Vegetable Puffs with Dipping Sauce, Minted Pea and Watercress Soup, Savoury Avocados with Pistachios (page 14), Spinach and Tomato Crepe Bake

SAVOURY AVOCADOS WITH PISTACHIOS

Avocado lovers will enjoy these tangy filled avocados as a starter or light meal. Make the filling in advance, but leave the assembly until shortly before serving.

Serves 6

- ☐ **3 avocados, halved and stoned**
- ☐ **1 tablespoon lemon juice**
- ☐ **2 tablespoons roughly chopped unsalted pistachio nuts**

FILLING
- ☐ **1 large zucchini (courgette), grated**
- ☐ **2 tablespoons finely chopped fresh mint**
- ☐ **2 tablespoons roughly chopped unsalted pistachio nuts**
- ☐ **2 tablespoons thick sour cream**
- ☐ **2 tablespoons lime juice**
- ☐ **freshly ground black pepper**

1 Brush cut surfaces of avocados with lemon juice, cover and set aside.
2 To make filling, place zucchini (courgette), mint and pistachios in a bowl. Whisk together sour cream and lime juice and pour into zucchini (courgette) mixture. Toss to combine. Season with pepper.
3 Spoon zucchini (courgette) filling into avocados and sprinkle with pistachios.

SPINACH TIMBALES WITH SPICY PEAR SAUCE

These deep green timbales look sensational when served with the pale Spicy Pear Sauce, and as a final touch, you might like to garnish the plate with a fanned pear slice! Great as a starter or light meal.

Serves 4

- ☐ **500 g (1 lb) spinach leaves, roughly chopped**
- ☐ **3 eggs**
- ☐ **125 mL (4 fl oz) cream (single)**
- ☐ **pinch ground (grated) nutmeg**
- ☐ **freshly ground black pepper**

SPICY PEAR SAUCE
- ☐ **2 ripe pears, peeled, cored and roughly chopped**
- ☐ **2 tablespoons cream (single)**
- ☐ **¹/₂ teaspoon chilli sauce**
- ☐ **pinch ground (grated) nutmeg**

1 Boil, steam or microwave spinach until tender. Refresh under cold running water and drain thoroughly. Squeeze spinach to remove excess liquid. Place in food processor or blender and process until smooth. Add eggs, cream, nutmeg and pepper to taste and process again until all ingredients are combined.
2 Spoon spinach mixture into four greased individual timbale moulds (125 mL/4 fl oz capacity), cover with foil and place in a baking dish. Pour in boiling water to come halfway up the sides of the moulds. Bake at 180°C (350°F/Gas 4) for 40-45 minutes or until set. Remove from water and leave 5 minutes before turning out.
3 To make sauce, place pears, cream, chilli sauce and nutmeg in food processor or blender and process until smooth. Transfer to a small saucepan and heat gently for 3-4 minutes, or until the sauce is just warm. Serve with timbales.

COOK'S TIP

If fresh pears are unavailable, canned pears in natural juice can be used as a substitute.

CORN AND CHILLI SOUFFLE

Serves 4

- ☐ **60 g (2 oz) polyunsaturated margarine**
- ☐ **1 onion, finely chopped**
- ☐ **1 red chilli, seeds removed and finely chopped**
- ☐ **3 tablespoons plain flour**
- ☐ **125 mL (4 fl oz) milk**
- ☐ **315 g (10 oz) canned creamed corn**
- ☐ **4 egg yolks, lightly beaten**
- ☐ **freshly ground black pepper**
- ☐ **5 egg whites**
- ☐ **3 tablespoons breadcrumbs made from stale bread**

1 Melt margarine in a saucepan and cook onion and chilli over a medium heat for 10 minutes, or until onion is soft and golden. Stir in flour and cook for 1 minute. Remove from heat and gradually stir in milk and corn. Return to heat and cook, stirring constantly, until mixture boils and thickens. Remove from heat and beat in egg yolks. Season to taste with pepper.
2 Place egg whites in a medium bowl and beat until stiff peaks form. Fold gently into corn mixture.
3 Grease an 18 cm (7 in) souffle dish and sprinkle with breadcrumbs. Grease a paper collar, sprinkle with breadcrumbs and attach to souffle dish.
4 Spoon souffle mixture into prepared dish and bake at 200°C (400°F/Gas 6) for 30-35 minutes or until puffed and browned. Serve immediately.

Dish Pillivuyt

Corn and Chilli Souffle

SWEET POTATO SOUP WITH GINGER AND LIME

Serves 4

- ☐ **30 g (1 oz) polyunsaturated margarine**
- ☐ **1 onion, finely chopped**
- ☐ **1 clove garlic, crushed**
- ☐ **1¹/₂ teaspoons finely grated fresh root ginger**
- ☐ **750 g (1¹/₂ lb) sweet potato, peeled and cut into chunks**
- ☐ **1 litre (1³/₄ pt) vegetable stock or water**
- ☐ **2 tablespoons lime juice**
- ☐ **ground white pepper**

1   Melt margarine in a saucepan and cook onion, garlic and ginger for 2-3 minutes or until soft. Add sweet potato and stock. Bring to the boil, then reduce heat and simmer for 15-20 minutes or until potato is tender.

2   Transfer to a food processor or blender with the lime juice and process until smooth. Return to a clean saucepan and reheat for 2-3 minutes. Season to taste with pepper. To serve, spoon into individual bowls.

SUMMER WHITE GAZPACHO

A deliciously different approach to the traditional gazpacho that can be prepared in advance for your next dinner party, or served as a refreshing start to a summer meal.

Serves 6

- ☐ **1 large green pepper, seeded and chopped**
- ☐ **1 cucumber, peeled, seeded and chopped**
- ☐ **1 red onion, chopped**
- ☐ **125 g (4 oz) breadcrumbs made from stale bread**
- ☐ **90 g (3 oz) ground almonds**
- ☐ **2 cloves garlic, crushed**
- ☐ **3 tablespoons olive oil**
- ☐ **1 teaspoon paprika**
- ☐ **¹/₂ teaspoon sugar**
- ☐ **1 tablespoon white wine vinegar**
- ☐ **750 mL (1¹/₄ pt) vegetable stock**
- ☐ **ground white pepper**
- ☐ **chopped green pepper, chopped cucumber and croutons to serve**

1   Place pepper, cucumber and onion in food processor or blender and process until smooth. Add breadcrumbs, almonds, garlic, oil, paprika, sugar, vinegar and vegetable stock and process until blended. Season to taste with pepper.

2   Transfer to a serving bowl, cover and refrigerate for 2 hours or until well chilled. To serve, top soup with chopped green pepper, cucumber and croutons.

SOUFFLE COLLARS

To make a paper collar, cut a piece of greaseproof paper 5 cm (2 in) longer than the circumference of the souffle dish. Fold in half lengthways to double the thickness. Wrap it around the souffle dish; it should extend about 5 cm (2 in) above the rim of the dish. Secure with string.

Sweet Potato Soup with Ginger and Lime, Summer White Gazpacho, Spinach Timbales with Spicy Pear Sauce

While 'grazing' is a delightful way to eat – snacking here, tasting there – there is no substitute for sitting down to a hearty main meal with family or friends.

MAIN EVENTS
with imagination

❖
CORN ROULADE WITH MUSHROOM FILLING

Serves 4

- ☐ 60 g (2 oz) polyunsaturated margarine
- ☐ 4 tablespoons wholemeal plain flour
- ☐ 185 mL (6 fl oz) milk
- ☐ 3 eggs, separated
- ☐ 125 g (4 oz) canned creamed corn

FILLING
- ☐ 90 mL (3 fl oz) vegetable stock or water
- ☐ 3 tablespoons thick sour cream or unflavoured yogurt
- ☐ 2 tablespoons chopped fresh basil
- ☐ 15 g ($^1/_2$ oz) polyunsaturated margarine
- ☐ 185 g (6 oz) mushrooms, finely chopped
- ☐ 1 onion, finely chopped
- ☐ 1 tablespoon plain flour

SAUCE
- ☐ 30 g (1 oz) polyunsaturated margarine
- ☐ 1 onion, chopped
- ☐ 2 teaspoons plain flour
- ☐ 250 mL (8 fl oz) vegetable stock or water
- ☐ 200 g ($6^1/_2$ oz) canned sweet red peppers, drained and chopped

1　Melt margarine in a saucepan, stir in flour and cook for 1 minute. Gradually blend in milk and cook over a medium heat, stirring frequently, until mixture boils and thickens. Whisk in egg yolks and corn. Whisk egg whites until stiff peaks form and gently fold through corn mixture. Spread mixture into a lightly greased and lined 25 x 30 cm (10 x 12 in) Swiss roll pan (tin). Bake at 220°C (425°F/Gas 7) for 15-20 minutes or until puffed and golden.

2　To make filling, whisk together stock, sour cream and basil. Melt margarine in a saucepan, add mushrooms and onion and cook for 5 minutes or until onion softens. Add flour and cook for 1 minute. Gradually stir in stock mixture and cook over a medium heat, stirring constantly until mixture boils and thickens.

3　To make sauce, melt margarine in a saucepan and cook onion for 3 minutes, stir in flour and cook for 1 minute longer. Gradually mix in stock and peppers and cook over a medium heat, stirring frequently until sauce boils and thickens.

4　Turn roulade onto a wire rack covered with a clean tea-towel and remove paper. Quickly spread with warm filling and gently roll up from the short side, with the help of the tea-towel. Serve roulade sliced with warm sauce.

❖❖
GINGERED VEGETABLES IN BREAD BASKETS

Serves 4

- ☐ vegetable oil for cooking
- ☐ 2 large pitta breads, split through centre

FILLING
- ☐ 8 baby potatoes, cut into bite-size pieces
- ☐ 1 carrot, chopped
- ☐ 1 zucchini (courgette), chopped
- ☐ 250 g (8 oz) snow peas (mange tout), topped and tailed
- ☐ 250 g (8 oz) green and yellow squash, trimmed and quartered
- ☐ 1 tablespoon grated root ginger
- ☐ 2 tablespoons honey
- ☐ 2 tablespoons orange juice
- ☐ 2 tablespoons chopped macadamia nuts, toasted
- ☐ 2 tablespoons finely snipped fresh chives

1　Heat oil in a wok or large saucepan and cook pitta breads one at a time. Press with the head of a metal soup ladle to form a basket. Drain on absorbent kitchen paper. Set aside and keep warm.

2　To make filling, boil, steam or microwave potatoes, carrot, zucchini (courgette), snow peas (mange tout) and squash separately until tender. Set aside and keep warm.

3　Combine ginger, honey, orange juice, nuts and chives in a large bowl. Add vegetables and toss to coat. Spoon filling into warm baskets and serve immediately.

❖
WARM BASIL SUMMER SALAD

Any small pasta with a good shape for catching the dressing can be used for this salad. You might like to try small shell pasta or small spiral shapes.

Serves 6

- ☐ 250 g (8 oz) small pasta shapes
- ☐ 2 tablespoons finely chopped sun-dried tomatoes
- ☐ $^1/_2$ red pepper, finely sliced
- ☐ $^1/_2$ green pepper, finely sliced
- ☐ 2 spring onions (shallots), chopped
- ☐ 12 black olives
- ☐ 2 tablespoons finely chopped basil
- ☐ 2 tablespoons grated Parmesan cheese

RED WINE VINEGAR DRESSING
- ☐ 1 clove garlic, crushed
- ☐ 1 tablespoon olive oil
- ☐ 3 tablespoons red wine vinegar
- ☐ $^1/_4$ teaspoon chilli powder
- ☐ freshly ground black pepper

1　Cook pasta in boiling water following packet instructions. Drain and set aside to keep warm.

2　Place tomatoes, red and green peppers, spring onions (shallots), olives and basil in a large salad bowl.

3　To make dressing, place garlic, oil, vinegar and chilli powder in a screw-top jar and shake well to combine. Season to taste with pepper.

4　Add warm pasta and dressing to salad bowl and toss lightly to combine. Sprinkle with Parmesan cheese and serve while pasta is still warm.

Gingered Vegetables in Bread Baskets, Warm Basil Summer Salad, Corn Roulade with Mushroom Filling

Plates Taitu

❖

LENTIL WONTONS WITH CORIANDER SAUCE

Makes 40

- ☐ **15 g (¹/2 oz) dried mushrooms, soaked in hot water for 10 minutes, drained and finely chopped**
- ☐ **100 g (3¹/2 oz) spinach, finely chopped**
- ☐ **1 tablespoon dry sherry**
- ☐ **60 g (2 oz) cabbage, finely chopped**
- ☐ **2 teaspoons soy sauce**
- ☐ **¹/2 teaspoon sesame oil**
- ☐ **2 teaspoons grated fresh root ginger**
- ☐ **4 spring onions (shallots), finely chopped**
- ☐ **75 g (2¹/2 oz) red lentils, cooked and drained**
- ☐ **40 prepared wonton or spring roll wrappers**
- ☐ **1 egg, lightly beaten with 60 mL (2 fl oz) water**
- ☐ **vegetable oil for cooking**

CORIANDER SAUCE

- ☐ **1 tablespoon white vinegar**
- ☐ **100 mL (3¹/2 fl oz) water**
- ☐ **1 teaspoon soy sauce**
- ☐ **3 tablespoons honey**
- ☐ **¹/2 teaspoon sesame oil**
- ☐ **¹/2 teaspoon grated fresh root ginger**
- ☐ **¹/2 teaspoon sweet chilli sauce**
- ☐ **2 teaspoons chopped fresh coriander**

1 Place mushrooms, spinach, sherry, cabbage, soy sauce, sesame oil, ginger, spring onions (shallots) and lentils in a bowl. Mix well to combine.

2 Place a teaspoon of mixture in the centre of each wonton wrapper. Brush the edges with egg mixture and gather up, pressing firmly together.

3 To make sauce, place vinegar, water, soy sauce, honey, sesame oil, ginger, chilli sauce and coriander in a small saucepan. Cook gently until heated through.

4 Heat oil in a large saucepan and cook wontons for 5 minutes or until golden and crisp. Serve wontons, with sauce for dipping.

DID YOU KNOW?
The Egyptians left dried beans in the pyramids of the Pharaohs as they believed the beans were helpful in conveying the soul to heaven.

❖

DOLMADES

Serves 20

- ☐ **375 g (12 oz) packaged vine leaves, rinsed**
- ☐ **500 mL (16 fl oz) vegetable stock, approximately**

FILLING
- ☐ **60 g (2 oz) brown rice, cooked**
- ☐ **60 g (2 oz) lentils, cooked**
- ☐ **2 spring onions (shallots), chopped**
- ☐ **1 small tomato, peeled and chopped**
- ☐ **2 tablespoons chopped pine nuts, toasted**
- ☐ **¹/2 teaspoon grated lemon rind**
- ☐ **1 tablespoon lemon juice**
- ☐ **2 teaspoons chopped fresh basil**
- ☐ **1 clove garlic, crushed**
- ☐ **2 teaspoons olive oil**

1 Place vine leaves in a saucepan, cover with water and set aside to stand for 5 minutes. Bring to the boil, drain and set aside to cool.

2 To make filling, place rice, lentils, spring onions (shallots), tomato, pine nuts, lemon peel, lemon juice, basil, garlic and oil in a bowl and mix well to combine.

3 Place teaspoonfuls of filling in the centre of each leaf and roll up tightly into neat parcels.

4 Place rolls close together in a large heavy-based saucepan or frypan and cover with any remaining vine leaves. Place a plate or saucer over the rolls to prevent them unrolling during cooking. Pour enough stock over the rolls to cover. Cover, bring to the boil, then reduce heat and simmer for 45 minutes.

❖

CURRIED LENTIL AND VEGETABLE SOUP

A thick and hearty soup to make ahead of time. Great for a main meal!

Serves 6

- ☐ **2 tablespoons vegetable oil**
- ☐ **1 onion, chopped**
- ☐ **2 teaspoons curry powder**
- ☐ **$^1/_2$ teaspoon ground cumin**
- ☐ **1 tablespoon concentrated tomato paste**
- ☐ **1.5 litres (2$^1/_2$ pt) vegetable stock**
- ☐ **125 g (4 oz) green or red lentils**
- ☐ **125 g (4 oz) broccoli, broken into small florets**
- ☐ **2 carrots, peeled and chopped**
- ☐ **1 parsnip, peeled and chopped**
- ☐ **1 stalk celery, chopped**
- ☐ **1 tablespoon chopped fresh parsley**

1 Heat oil in a large saucepan and cook onion, curry powder and cumin for 4-5 minutes, or until onion softens. Stir in tomato paste and stock and bring to the boil, stirring occasionally. Reduce heat, add lentils, cover and simmer for 30 minutes.

2 Add broccoli, carrots, parsnip and celery, cover and cook for 30 minutes longer or until vegetables are tender. Just prior to serving stir in parsley.

Left: Lentil Wontons with Coriander Sauce, Dolmades
Right: Curried Lentil and Vegetable Soup, Italian-Style Winter Vegetable Soup

❖

ITALIAN-STYLE WINTER VEGETABLE SOUP

A hearty meal in itself that will satisfy even the most hungry members of your family. Delicious with freshly chopped parsley, Parmesan cheese and crusty bread.

Serves 6

- ☐ **2 tablespoons vegetable oil**
- ☐ **1 large onion, sliced**
- ☐ **1 clove garlic, crushed**
- ☐ **2 stalks celery, chopped**
- ☐ **2 carrots, chopped**
- ☐ **1 turnip, peeled and chopped**
- ☐ **440 g (14 oz) canned peeled tomatoes, undrained and mashed**
- ☐ **2 tablespoons concentrated tomato paste**
- ☐ **1 tablespoon finely chopped fresh basil**
- ☐ **1 teaspoon dried oregano**
- ☐ **1 teaspoon sugar**
- ☐ **1.5 litres (2$^1/_2$ pt) vegetable stock**
- ☐ **125 g (4 oz) small pasta shells**
- ☐ **315 g (10 oz) canned red kidney beans, drained and rinsed**
- ☐ **freshly ground black pepper**

1 Heat oil in a large saucepan and cook onion, garlic, celery, carrots and turnip for 4-5 minutes or until vegetables are just tender.

2 Stir in tomatoes, tomato paste, basil, oregano, sugar and stock. Bring to the boil, reduce heat and simmer for 30-45 minutes.

3 Stir in pasta and beans. Season to taste with pepper and simmer, uncovered, for 30 minutes. To serve, spoon into individual bowls.

Tiles Country Floors China Pillivuyt

BAKED POTATOES

✧ Baked potatoes are terrific when accompanied with a crisp, green salad. They make a satisfying meal that the whole family will enjoy again and again.

✧ These fillings will be enough to fill six medium potato shells. Just increase or decrease the quantity of filling according to the number of potatoes you wish to fill.

✧ Try these combinations for starters, then be adventurous, and try your own. You will find that there are endless ways to fill a potato!

✧ To cook potatoes, scrub well and bake at 180°C (350°F/Gas 4) for 45 minutes, or microwave on HIGH (100%) for 10 minutes per 500 g (1 lb), or until potatoes are tender.

Potatoes with tasty fillings from left to right: Curried Cauliflower and Sultana, Mushroom, Sour Cream and Grain Mustard, Asparagus, Avocado and Tarragon, Grilled Pepper, Garlic and Parsley, Spinach and Cheese

❖

MUSHROOM, SOUR CREAM AND GRAIN MUSTARD

Serves 6

- ☐ **6 potatoes, baked in their jackets**

FILLING
- ☐ **15 g (^{1}/2 oz) butter**
- ☐ **125 g (4 oz) button mushrooms, sliced**
- ☐ **125 g (4 oz) thick sour cream**
- ☐ **2 teaspoons wholegrain mustard**
- ☐ **2 teaspoons snipped chives**
- ☐ **60 g (2 oz) tasty cheese, grated**

1 Cut tops from potatoes. Scoop out flesh with a spoon leaving a 1 cm (^{1}/2 in) thick shell. Place flesh in a bowl and set aside.

2 To make filling, melt butter in a saucepan and cook mushrooms for 1-2 minutes. Mash potato flesh with sour cream and mustard. Fold in mushrooms and chives.

3 Spoon mixture into potato shells and sprinkle with cheese. Bake at 180°C (350°F/Gas 4) for 10-15 minutes or until golden.

❖

ASPARAGUS, AVOCADO AND TARRAGON

Serves 6

- ☐ **6 potatoes, baked in their jackets**

FILLING
- ☐ **300 g (9^1/2 oz) fresh asparagus, cut into 2.5 cm (1 in) pieces**
- ☐ **2 tablespoons tarragon vinegar**
- ☐ **1 teaspoon dried tarragon**
- ☐ **2 tablespoons lemon juice**
- ☐ **100 g (3^1/2 oz) grated tasty cheese**
- ☐ **1 avocado, stoned, peeled and cut into 2.5 cm (1 in) cubes**
- ☐ **freshly ground black pepper**

1 Cut tops from potatoes. Scoop out flesh with a spoon leaving a 1 cm (^{1}/2 in) thick shell. Reserve flesh for other use and keep shells warm.

2 To make filling, boil, steam or microwave asparagus until tender. Combine vinegar, tarragon and lemon juice in a saucepan and boil until reduced by half. Remove from heat and gently stir in asparagus, cheese and avocado. Spoon filling into potato shells, and bake at 180°C (350°F/Gas 4) for 10-15 minutes.

CURRIED CAULIFLOWER AND SULTANA

Serves 6

- [ ] **6 potatoes, baked in their jackets**

FILLING
- [ ] **1 tablespoon olive oil**
- [ ] **$^1/_2$ teaspoon cumin seeds**
- [ ] **$^1/_2$ teaspoon ground coriander**
- [ ] **1 small red chilli, finely chopped**
- [ ] **$^1/_4$ teaspoon ground turmeric**
- [ ] **155 g (5 oz) cauliflower, cut into small florets**
- [ ] **60 g (2 oz) sultanas**
- [ ] **90 g (3 oz) unflavoured yogurt**

1   Cut tops from potatoes. Scoop out flesh with a spoon leaving a 1 cm ($^1/_2$ in) thick shell. Reserve flesh and place in a mixing bowl. Keep shells warm.

2   To make filling, heat oil in a frypan and cook cumin, coriander, chilli and turmeric for 1 minute. Add cauliflower, toss to coat with spice mixture and cook for 6-8 minutes or until tender. Mash potato flesh. Combine potato, sultanas and yogurt with cauliflower mixture. Spoon into the potato shells and serve.

SPINACH AND CHEESE

Serves 6

- [ ] **6 potatoes, baked in their jackets**

FILLING
- [ ] **1 tablespoon olive oil**
- [ ] **1 onion, finely sliced**
- [ ] **6 large English spinach leaves, stalks removed and leaves finely shredded**
- [ ] **3 hard-boiled eggs, finely chopped**
- [ ] **60 g (2 oz) blue cheese, crumbled**
- [ ] **4 tablespoons thick sour cream**
- [ ] **freshly ground black pepper**

1   Cut tops from potatoes. Scoop out flesh with a spoon leaving a 1 cm ($^1/_2$ in) thick shell. Reserve flesh for another use and keep shells warm.

2   To make filling, heat oil in a frypan and cook onion until crisp and golden. Drain on absorbent kitchen paper. Combine onion, spinach and eggs. Set aside.

3   Combine blue cheese and sour cream in a mixing bowl and beat until smooth and slightly runny. Season to taste with pepper.

4   Fill potato shells with spinach mixture. Top with blue cheese mixture and serve.

GRILLED PEPPER, GARLIC AND PARSLEY

Serves 6

- [ ] **6 potatoes, baked in their jackets**

FILLING
- [ ] **2 red peppers, cut into quarters**
- [ ] **1 green pepper, cut into quarters**
- [ ] **2 cloves garlic, crushed**
- [ ] **2 teaspoons olive oil**
- [ ] **2 tablespoons chopped fresh flat leaf parsley**
- [ ] **2 tablespoons grated mozzarella cheese**

1   Cut tops from potatoes. Scoop out flesh with a spoon leaving a 1 cm ($^1/_2$ in) thick shell. Place flesh in a bowl and set aside.

2   Grill red and green peppers until skin blisters. Peel and slice thinly. Mash potato flesh with garlic, oil and parsley. Fold through peppers and spoon into potato shells. Sprinkle with mozzarella and bake at 180°C (350°F/Gas 4) for 10 minutes or until cheese melts and is golden.

❖

SUMMER FRITTATA

Serves 6

- ☐ **30 g (1 oz) polyunsaturated margarine**
- ☐ **1 clove garlic, crushed**
- ☐ **4 zucchini (courgettes), sliced**
- ☐ **8 eggs, lightly beaten**
- ☐ **2 tablespoons chopped sun-dried tomatoes**
- ☐ **6 spring onions (shallots), finely chopped**
- ☐ **1 tablespoon chopped fresh basil**
- ☐ **1 tablespoon chopped fresh mint**
- ☐ **freshly ground black pepper**
- ☐ **30 g (1 oz) grated tasty cheese**

1 Melt margarine in a large frypan and cook garlic and zucchini (courgettes) over a medium heat for 5-6 minutes, or until zucchini (courgettes) are just tender.

2 Place eggs, tomatoes, spring onions (shallots), basil and mint in a bowl and mix to combine. Season to taste with pepper. Pour over zucchini (courgettes) in pan and gently move vegetables to allow the egg mixture to run under. Reduce heat to low and cook until frittata is brown on the base and just set.

3 Slide onto an oven tray, sprinkle with cheese and place under a preheated grill for 4-5 minutes or until cheese melts and is golden. Serve hot, warm or at room temperature, cut into wedges.

❖

RISOTTO PRIMAVERA

Serves 8

- ☐ **410 g (13 oz) yellow baby squash, cut into quarters**
- ☐ **4 zucchini (courgettes), thickly sliced**
- ☐ **2 red peppers, seeds removed and cut into quarters**
- ☐ **250 g (8 oz) fresh asparagus cut into 2.5 cm (1 in) pieces**
- ☐ **freshly ground black pepper**
- ☐ **3 tablespoons grated fresh Parmesan cheese**

RISOTTO
- ☐ **125 g (4 oz) butter**
- ☐ **2 leeks, sliced**
- ☐ **2 cloves garlic, crushed**
- ☐ **500 g (1 lb) Arborio rice**
- ☐ **250 mL (8 fl oz) dry white wine**
- ☐ **3 tablespoons tarragon vinegar**
- ☐ **2 bay leaves**
- ☐ **750 mL (1¼ pt) vegetable stock**
- ☐ **6 sun-dried tomatoes, chopped**
- ☐ **1 tablespoon chopped fresh basil**
- ☐ **freshly ground black pepper**

1 To make risotto, melt butter in a heavy-based saucepan and cook leeks and garlic until soft and transparent. Stir in rice, tossing well to coat with butter.

2 Stir in wine and vinegar and simmer until most of liquid is absorbed. Add bay leaves and 500 mL (16 fl oz) stock. Simmer until liquid is absorbed. Stir in sun-dried tomatoes and remaining stock. Simmer, stirring frequently, until liquid is almost absorbed and rice is tender. Stir in basil.

3 Boil, steam or microwave squash, zucchini (courgettes) and asparagus separately until tender. Set aside and keep warm. Grill peppers, skin side up until skin blisters. Peel and slice thickly. Toss vegetables together and season to taste with black pepper. To serve, place risotto on a serving plate and surround with vegetables. Sprinkle with Parmesan cheese.

Cheese and Onion Bread Pudding, Risotto Primavera

Plates Villeroy & Boch Dish Pillivuyt

CHEESY TOFU AND VEGETABLE STRUDEL

Serves 6

- ☐ **12 sheets filo pastry**
- ☐ **45 g (1¹/2 oz) polyunsaturated margarine, melted**
- ☐ **2 teaspoons grated Parmesan cheese**
- ☐ **2 teaspoons sesame seeds**

FILLING

- ☐ **200 g (6¹/2 oz) fresh asparagus, chopped**
- ☐ **2 carrots, grated**
- ☐ **2 potatoes, grated**
- ☐ **3 tablespoons concentrated tomato paste**
- ☐ **350 g (11 oz) silken tofu, cut into 1 cm (¹/2 in) cubes**
- ☐ **3 tablespoons chopped fresh basil**
- ☐ **100 g (3¹/2 oz) grated tasty cheese**
- ☐ **3 tablespoons thick sour cream**
- ☐ **freshly ground black pepper**

1 To make filling, boil, steam or microwave asparagus, carrots and potatoes separately until just tender. Drain. Place cooked vegetables, tomato paste, tofu, basil, cheese and sour cream in a bowl and mix well to combine. Season to taste with pepper. Divide mixture in half.

2 Layer 6 pastry sheets, brushing each sheet with melted margarine. Spoon one half of vegetable mixture along one long edge of pastry, leaving a 7.5 cm (3 in) border, fold in edges and roll up carefully like a Swiss roll. Repeat with remaining pastry and mixture.

3 Carefully lift strudels onto a lightly oiled baking tray (sheet), brush top with any remaining margarine and sprinkle with Parmesan cheese and sesame seeds. Bake at 180°C (350°F/Gas 4) for 25 minutes or until golden.

CHEESE AND ONION BREAD PUDDING

Serves 6

- ☐ **30 g (1 oz) polyunsaturated margarine**
- ☐ **3 large onions, finely sliced**
- ☐ **¹/2 teaspoon dried thyme**
- ☐ **60 g (2 oz) grated Parmesan cheese**
- ☐ **60 g (2 oz) grated smoked cheese**
- ☐ **125 g (4 oz) grated tasty cheese**
- ☐ **1 tablespoon snipped fresh chives**
- ☐ **8 slices wholemeal bread, crusts removed**
- ☐ **3 eggs, lightly beaten**
- ☐ **500 mL (16 fl oz) milk**
- ☐ **freshly ground black pepper**

1 Heat margarine in a frypan and cook onions and thyme over a gentle heat for 10-15 minutes, or until onions are golden and soft.

2 Combine Parmesan, smoked and tasty cheeses with chives. Place half the bread slices in a greased baking dish, cutting slices to fit snugly, if necessary. Cover with onion mixture and sprinkle with half the cheese mixture. Repeat with remaining bread and cheese.

3 Place eggs and milk in a bowl and whisk to combine. Season to taste with pepper. Pour over bread and cheese in baking dish and bake at 190°C (375°F/Gas 5) for 30-35 minutes, or until custard is firm and golden.

Cheesy Tofu and Vegetable Strudel, Summer Frittata

SWEET AND SOUR RICE BALLS

Makes 16

- ☐ 30 g (1 oz) polyunsaturated margarine
- ☐ 315 g (10 oz) short-grain rice
- ☐ 4 spring onions (shallots), finely chopped
- ☐ 2 teaspoons grated fresh root ginger
- ☐ 750 mL (1^1/$_4$ pt) vegetable stock
- ☐ 155 g (5 oz) grated tasty cheese
- ☐ 1 egg, lightly beaten
- ☐ plain flour
- ☐ 1 egg, beaten with 60 mL (2 fl oz) milk
- ☐ 200 g (6^1/$_2$ oz) wholemeal bread-crumbs made from stale bread
- ☐ vegetable oil for cooking

SWEET AND SOUR SAUCE

- ☐ 4 dried mushrooms, soaked in hot water for 10 minutes, drained and finely chopped
- ☐ 220 g (7 oz) canned pineapple pieces, chopped and liquid reserved
- ☐ 4 spring onions (shallots), finely chopped
- ☐ 2 teaspoons Hoisin sauce
- ☐ 1 tablespoon white vinegar
- ☐ 250 mL (8 fl oz) water blended with 1 tablespoon cornflour
- ☐ 1 teaspoon sambal oelek
- ☐ 2 teaspoons soy sauce
- ☐ 2 teaspoons tamarind paste

1   Melt margarine in a saucepan, stir in rice, spring onions (shallots) and ginger and cook, stirring frequently, for 2 minutes. Pour in vegetable stock and bring to the boil, stirring occasionally. Reduce heat, cover with a tight-fitting lid and simmer for 20 minutes, or until rice is tender and liquid absorbed. Remove from heat and set aside to cool. Mix in cheese and egg.

2   Spread mixture in a lightly oiled 20 x 30 cm (8 x 12 in) shallow pan (tin), cover and refrigerate until firm.

3   To make sauce, combine mushrooms, pineapple, 60 mL (2 fl oz) reserved pineapple liquid, spring onions (shallots), Hoisin sauce, vinegar, cornflour mixture, sambal oelek, soy sauce and tamarind paste in a saucepan. Cook over a medium heat until mixture boils and thickens.

4   Divide rice mixture into sixteen portions and roll into balls. Toss balls in flour, dip in egg mixture and roll in breadcrumbs.

5   Heat oil in a large saucepan and cook a few balls at a time for 3-4 minutes or until golden. Drain on absorbent kitchen paper and serve with sauce.

POLENTA CROQUETTES WITH TOMATO SAUCE

The sharp tang of chillies combines well with mint in this tomato-based sauce.

Makes 12

- ☐ 1 litre (1^3/$_4$ pt) vegetable stock or water
- ☐ 200 g (6^1/$_2$ oz) polenta
- ☐ 4 spring onions (shallots), finely chopped
- ☐ 1 stalk celery, finely chopped
- ☐ ^{1}/$_2$ small red pepper, finely chopped
- ☐ plain flour
- ☐ 2 eggs, lightly beaten with 125 mL (4 fl oz) milk
- ☐ 200 g (6^1/$_2$ oz) wholemeal breadcrumbs made from stale bread mixed with 1 teaspoon ground cumin
- ☐ vegetable oil for cooking

TOMATO SAUCE

- ☐ 440 g (14 oz) canned peeled tomatoes, undrained and mashed
- ☐ 2 tablespoons finely chopped fresh mint
- ☐ 2 teaspoons curry powder
- ☐ 2 small red chillies, finely chopped

1   Place vegetable stock in a large saucepan and bring to the boil, then stir in polenta. Cover and simmer for 30 minutes or until thick. Add spring onions (shallots), celery and pepper and mix well. Spread into a lightly oiled 30 x 20 cm (12 x 8 in) shallow pan (tin). Set aside to stand for 2 hours.

2   Cut polenta into fingers, toss in flour, dip in egg mixture and then in breadcrumb mixture. Refrigerate for 15 minutes or until required.

3   To make sauce, combine tomatoes, mint, curry powder and chillies in a saucepan. Bring to the boil and cook stirring for 5 minutes or until sauce thickens.

4   Heat oil in a large saucepan and cook polenta fingers a few at a time for 3-4 minutes or until golden. Drain on absorbent kitchen paper and serve with sauce.

THAI-STYLE VEGETARIAN CURRY

A spicy, fragrant curry – delicious when served with jasmine or saffron-flavoured rice.

Serves 6

- ☐ 2 tablespoons peanut oil
- ☐ 2 onions, sliced
- ☐ 2 cloves garlic, crushed
- ☐ 2 small red chillies, finely chopped
- ☐ 2 teaspoons grated fresh root ginger
- ☐ 2 tablespoons chopped fresh coriander
- ☐ 1 teaspoon ground cumin
- ☐ 1 tablespoon red curry paste
- ☐ 1 small head cauliflower, cut into florets
- ☐ 3 large potatoes, peeled and roughly chopped
- ☐ 1 eggplant (aubergine), cut into 2.5 cm (1 in) pieces
- ☐ 2 carrots, peeled and thickly sliced
- ☐ 4 zucchini (courgettes), roughly chopped
- ☐ 3 tablespoons fish sauce
- ☐ 440 g (14 oz) canned coconut cream
- ☐ 2 tablespoons chopped fresh basil
- ☐ 1 teaspoon grated lime rind

1   Heat oil in a saucepan and cook onions, garlic, chillies, ginger, coriander and cumin for 5 minutes, or until onions soften. Stir in curry paste, cauliflower, potatoes, eggplant (aubergine) and carrots, and cook for 2-3 minutes longer. Toss vegetables to coat with spices.

2   Mix in zucchini (courgettes), fish sauce, coconut cream, basil and lime rind, cover and simmer, stirring occasionally, for 15 minutes, or until vegetables are tender and sauce thickens slightly.

From left: Sweet and Sour Rice Balls, Polenta Croquettes with Tomato Sauce, Savoury Pumpkin Flan, Thai-Style Vegetarian Curry, Spinach Timbales with Pasta Filling

SAVOURY PUMPKIN FLAN

Serves 4

- ☐ **4 sheets filo pastry**
- ☐ **2 tablespoons vegetable oil**
- ☐ **1 onion, chopped**
- ☐ **250 g (8 oz) pumpkin, peeled, seeded, cooked and mashed**
- ☐ **185 g (6 oz) grated tasty cheese**
- ☐ **2 eggs, separated**
- ☐ **2 tablespoons thick sour cream or unflavoured yogurt**
- ☐ **freshly ground black pepper**
- ☐ **pinch chilli powder**
- ☐ **1 tablespoon chopped fresh parsley**

1 Brush each sheet of pastry with oil and fold in half. Layer pastry, one folded piece on top of the other, to give eight layers. Place an 18 cm (7 in) flan dish upside down on the layered pastry and cut around dish making a circle 5 cm (2 in) larger. Lift all layers of pastry into flan dish and roll down edges.

2 Heat remaining oil in a frypan and cook onion for 3-4 minutes or until soft. Combine onion, pumpkin, cheese, egg yolks and sour cream. Season to taste with pepper and chilli powder.

3 Whisk egg whites until stiff peaks form. Fold into pumpkin mixture and spoon into pastry case. Sprinkle with parsley. Bake at 200°C (400°F/Gas 6) for 30 minutes.

SPINACH TIMBALES WITH PASTA FILLING

Serves 4

- ☐ **6 large English spinach leaves, washed and stalks removed**

FILLING
- ☐ **2 tablespoons olive oil**
- ☐ **2 small eggplants (aubergines), chopped**
- ☐ **1 onion, chopped**
- ☐ **1 clove garlic, crushed**
- ☐ **1 red pepper, chopped**
- ☐ **2 zucchini (courgettes), chopped**
- ☐ **1 large ripe tomato, peeled and chopped**
- ☐ **2 tablespoons concentrated tomato paste**
- ☐ **1 teaspoon hot chilli powder**
- ☐ **3 tablespoons finely chopped pitted black olives**
- ☐ **4 tablespoons risoni pasta, cooked**
- ☐ **3 tablespoons grated Parmesan cheese**
- ☐ **freshly ground black pepper**

1 Boil, steam or microwave spinach until wilted. Drain well. Line four greased individual ramekins (250 mL/8 fl oz capacity) with spinach. Allow some leaves to overhang top.

2 To make filling, heat oil in a saucepan and cook eggplants (aubergines), onion, garlic, pepper, zucchini (courgettes) and tomato, stirring occasionally, for 15 minutes or until mixture thickens. Add tomato paste, chilli powder, olives, pasta and Parmesan cheese. Season to taste with pepper and mix well to combine.

3 Spoon filling into lined ramekins, fold overhanging leaves over filling and cover with greased foil. Bake at 180°C (350°F/Gas 4) for 20 minutes. Allow to stand for 5-10 minutes before turning out.

TOFU AND PEANUT BURGERS

Serves 6

- [ ] **6 wholegrain rolls, split and toasted**
- [ ] **6 lettuce leaves**
- [ ] **6 slices cooked beetroot**
- [ ] **2 hard-boiled eggs, chopped**
- [ ] **60 g (2 oz) thick sour cream**

TOFU AND NUT PATTIES
- [ ] **250 g (8 oz) silken tofu, drained**
- [ ] **2 carrots, grated and squeezed of excess liquid**
- [ ] **2 zucchini (courgettes), grated and squeezed of excess liquid**
- [ ] **60 g (2 oz) unsalted, roasted peanuts, finely chopped**
- [ ] **60 g (2 oz) walnuts, finely chopped**
- [ ] **125 g (4 oz) wholemeal breadcrumbs made from stale bread**
- [ ] **$^1/_2$ teaspoon ground fenugreek**
- [ ] **1 teaspoon ground coriander**
- [ ] **freshly ground black pepper**
- [ ] **2 tablespoons sesame seeds**
- [ ] **2 tablespoons poppy seeds**
- [ ] **2 tablespoons vegetable oil**

1   To make patties, mash tofu in a large bowl, stir in carrots, zucchini (courgettes), peanuts, walnuts, breadcrumbs, fenugreek and coriander. Season to taste with pepper. Combine sesame and poppy seeds. Shape mixture into six patties and roll in seeds.
2   Heat oil in a frypan and cook patties for 4-5 minutes on each side, or until crisp and golden brown.
3   Top base of each roll with a lettuce leaf, then a pattie, beetroot slice, spoonful of egg and a spoonful of sour cream. Replace top of roll and serve immediately.

TASTY FILO TRIANGLES

Makes 30

- [ ] **18 sheets filo pastry**
- [ ] **90 g (3 oz) polyunsaturated margarine, melted**
- [ ] **2 tablespoons grated Parmesan cheese**

FILLING
- [ ] **315 g (10 oz) yellow split peas**
- [ ] **1 tablespoon olive oil**
- [ ] **$^1/_2$ teaspoon ground cumin**
- [ ] **$^1/_4$ teaspoon ground coriander**
- [ ] **1 clove garlic, crushed**
- [ ] **2 teaspoons grated fresh root ginger**
- [ ] **1 small fresh red chilli, finely chopped**
- [ ] **2 tablespoons concentrated tomato paste**
- [ ] **1 teaspoon grated lemon rind**
- [ ] **315 g (10 oz) mushrooms, finely chopped**
- [ ] **250 g (8 oz) cottage cheese**
- [ ] **2 tablespoons snipped fresh chives**
- [ ] **freshly ground black pepper**

1   To make filling, cover peas with water and set aside to stand overnight. Drain and rinse well. Place peas in a saucepan of boiling water and cook for 20 minutes or until soft. Drain and set aside to cool.
2   Heat oil in a saucepan and cook cumin, coriander, garlic, ginger, chilli, tomato paste and lemon peel for 1-2 minutes. Add peas and mushrooms and cook, stirring frequently, for 10 minutes, or until most of the liquid has evaporated. Stir in cottage cheese and chives. Season with pepper.
3   Layer 3 pastry sheets together, brushing each sheet with margarine. Cut pastry crossways into six equal strips. Place teaspoonfuls of pea mixture on one end of each strip. Fold corner of pastry over filling to form a triangle shape. Lift first triangle up and over and continue folding to end of strip. Repeat with remaining pastry, margarine and pea mixture.
4   Place triangles on a baking tray (sheet), brush with remaining margarine and sprinkle with Parmesan cheese. Bake at 220°C (425°F/Gas 7) for 15 minutes or until golden.

MARINATED TOFU AND VEGETABLE SATAYS

Great for a vegetarian barbeque.

Serves 6

- [ ] **250 g (8 oz) button mushrooms**
- [ ] **12 pickling onions**
- [ ] **2 green peppers, cut into pieces**
- [ ] **12 baby yellow squash**
- [ ] **2 red peppers, cut into pieces**
- [ ] **1 eggplant (aubergine), cut into cubes**
- [ ] **250 g (8 oz) silken tofu, cut into cubes**

MARINADE
- [ ] **125 mL (4 oz) soy sauce**
- [ ] **60 mL (2 oz) dry sherry**
- [ ] **2 tablespoons honey**

SATAY SAUCE

- ☐ **220 g (7 oz) crunchy peanut butter**
- ☐ **1 small red chilli, finely chopped**
- ☐ **2 cloves garlic, crushed**
- ☐ **220 mL (7 fl oz) water**
- ☐ **1 tablespoon brown sugar**
- ☐ **2 teaspoons soy sauce**
- ☐ **1 tablespoon lemon juice**

1 To make marinade, combine soy sauce, sherry and honey in a flat dish. Thread mushrooms, onions, green pepper, squash, red pepper, eggplant (aubergine) and tofu onto twelve oiled wooden skewers and place in marinade. Cover and set aside for 30 minutes, turning once.

2 Remove skewers from marinade and cook under a preheated grill, or on a barbecue, for 10 minutes or until vegetables are tender. Brush frequently with marinade during cooking.

3 To make sauce, combine peanut butter, chilli, garlic, water, sugar, soy sauce and lemon juice in a saucepan and cook over a low heat for 10 minutes. If sauce becomes too thick add a little more water or lemon juice. Spoon sauce over skewers and serve immediately.

❖

CHEESY MUSHROOM AND ZUCCHINI (COURGETTE) BAKE

Served with a crisp, garden salad for a tasty meal, this simply prepared dish has a crunchy, sesame seed topping.

Serves 6

- ☐ **60 g (2 oz) butter**
- ☐ **2 onions, roughly chopped**
- ☐ **2 cloves garlic, crushed**
- ☐ **1 carrot, grated**
- ☐ **3 zucchini (courgettes), grated**
- ☐ **315 g (10 oz) mushrooms, sliced**
- ☐ **3 eggs, lightly beaten**
- ☐ **2 tablespoons plain flour**
- ☐ **2 tablespoons chopped fresh parsley**
- ☐ **60 g (2 oz) grated tasty cheese**
- ☐ **freshly ground black pepper**

TOPPING

- ☐ **60 g (2 oz) grated tasty cheese**
- ☐ **1 tablespoon sesame seeds**

1 Melt butter in a saucepan and cook onions and garlic for 2-3 minutes or until onions are soft. In a large bowl combine onion mixture, carrot, zucchini (courgettes), mushrooms, eggs, flour, parsley and cheese. Season to taste with pepper. Spoon mixture into a lightly greased 18 cm (7 in) springform pan (tin).

2 To make topping, combine cheese and sesame seeds and sprinkle over vegetable mixture. Bake at 180°C (350°F/ Gas 4) for 30 minutes or until firm and golden. Allow to stand 5-10 minutes before removing from pan (tin).

DID YOU KNOW?

Battle Creek, Michigan, USA was where breakfast cereals, peanut butter and vegetable protein foods all originated. The development of these foods goes back to Dr John Harvey Kellogg who was the medical director of the Seventh Day Adventist Health Reform Institute, later to be known as Battle Creek Sanitarium

---

Left: Tofu and Peanut Burgers
Above: Tasty Filo Triangles, Cheesy Mushroom and Zucchini (Courgette) Bake, Marinated Tofu and Vegetable Satays

You walk in late, and everyone is waiting for dinner. What to cook? In this section you will find delicious recipes that can be whipped up in minutes.

HOME LATE
dinner can't wait

❖

VEGETABLE AND NUT STIR-FRY

Serves 6

- ☐ **2 tablespoons vegetable oil**
- ☐ **2 onions, cut into eighths**
- ☐ **2 carrots, cut into thin strips**
- ☐ **2 stalks celery, cut into thin strips**
- ☐ **2 teaspoons turmeric**
- ☐ **2 cloves garlic, crushed**
- ☐ **6 spring onions (shallots), chopped**
- ☐ **2 tablespoons white vinegar**
- ☐ **2 tablespoons sugar**
- ☐ **1 mango, stoned, peeled and chopped**
- ☐ **125 g (4 oz) snow peas (mange tout), trimmed**
- ☐ **185 mL (6 fl oz) vegetable stock**
- ☐ **125 g (4 oz) roasted cashew nuts**

1   Heat oil in a wok or frypan. Add onions, carrots and celery and stir-fry for 5 minutes or until lightly browned. Combine turmeric, garlic, spring onions (shallots), vinegar and sugar and stir into wok.
2   Add mango, snow peas (mange tout) and stock and stir-fry for 5 minutes, or until vegetables are just tender. Fold through nuts and serve immediately.

BALSAMIC VINEGAR

Balsamic vinegar is a dark Italian vinegar made by the special processing of wines and musts from the Modena province. It is an interesting addition to any salad dressing, and can also be used in sauces for meats or vegetables. Balsamic vinegar is available from delicatessens and some supermarkets.

❖

WARM RED CABBAGE SALAD

Make this wonderful warm salad in Autumn when apples and red cabbage are plentiful and at their best.

Serves 6

- ☐ **1 tablespoon olive oil**
- ☐ **1 clove garlic, crushed**
- ☐ **1 red onion, thinly sliced**
- ☐ **2 tablespoons balsamic vinegar**
- ☐ **1/2 small red cabbage, shredded**
- ☐ **2 green apples, peeled, cored and thinly sliced**
- ☐ **1 tablespoon finely snipped fresh chives**
- ☐ **1 tablespoon finely chopped fresh dill**
- ☐ **60 g (2 oz) slivered almonds, toasted**
- ☐ **60 g (2 oz) feta cheese, crumbled**

1   Heat oil in a large frypan. Add garlic and onion and cook over a medium heat for 2-3 minutes. Stir in vinegar and cook for 1 minute longer.
2   Add cabbage to pan, toss lightly and cook for 4-5 minutes, or until cabbage just starts to wilt and change colour. Transfer all contents of the pan to a salad bowl. Toss through apples, chives and dill. Sprinkle top of the salad with almonds and cheese and serve while salad is still warm.

Warm Red Cabbage Salad, Blue Cheese and Apple Omelette, Vegetable and Nut Stir-Fry

Plates Made In Japan

DID YOU KNOW?

✧ Apples were gathered by Stone Age man and were cultivated by the ancient Greeks, Romans and Egyptians.

✧ There are more than 7000 varieties of apples in the world today.

✧ If peeled apples are soaked in cold water with a tablespoon of lemon juice for 15 minutes they remain pale when cooked.

✧ The easiest way to slice apples neatly is to core them first, then peel, halve and finally cut them into even slices.

❖

BLUE CHEESE AND APPLE OMELETTE

Cheese and apples are natural partners, but as a filling in this omelette, they are an extra-special combination.

Serves 1

☐ **15 g (¹/₂ oz) polyunsaturated margarine**
☐ **2 eggs**
☐ **2 teaspoons water**
☐ **freshly ground black pepper**

FILLING
☐ **15 g (¹/₂ oz) polyunsaturated margarine**
☐ **¹/₂ small green apple, cored and thinly sliced**
☐ **30 g (1 oz) blue cheese, crumbled**
☐ **1 teaspoon finely snipped chives**

1 To make filling, melt margarine in a small frypan and cook apple over a gentle heat for 2-3 minutes or until just heated through. Remove from pan and set aside to keep warm.

2 To make omelette, melt margarine in a small frypan. Lightly whisk together eggs and water. Season to taste with pepper and pour into pan. Cook over a medium heat, continually drawing in the edge of the omelette with a fork during cooking, until no liquid remains and the omelette is lightly set.

3 Top omelette with apple slices, blue cheese and chives and fold in half. Slip onto a plate and serve immediately.

RICE FRITTERS

Serve with hummus or minted yogurt.

Makes 20

- [ ] $^1/_4$ teaspoon chilli powder
- [ ] 1 teaspoon garam masala
- [ ] 75 g ($2^1/_2$ oz) wholemeal plain flour
- [ ] 75 g ($2^1/_2$ oz) besan flour
- [ ] 125 g (4 oz) brown rice, cooked
- [ ] 2 eggs, lightly beaten with 185 mL (6 fl oz) milk
- [ ] 4 spring onions (shallots), finely chopped
- [ ] $^1/_2$ small red pepper, finely chopped
- [ ] vegetable oil for cooking

1 Sift chilli powder, garam masala and wholemeal and besan flours into a bowl. Mix in rice, make a well in the centre and gradually stir in egg mixture. Mix to a smooth batter and stir in spring onions (shallots) and pepper.

2 Heat oil in a frypan and cook spoonfuls of batter for 3-4 minutes or until golden each side. Drain on absorbent kitchen paper and serve.

RAINBOW FRITTATA WITH COCONUT CREAM

Serves 6

- [ ] 100 g ($3^1/_2$ oz) dried yellow mung beans, soaked in water overnight
- [ ] 2 eggs
- [ ] 2 tablespoons vegetable oil
- [ ] 1 onion, sliced
- [ ] 2 potatoes, peeled and grated
- [ ] 2 carrots, grated
- [ ] 2 zucchini (courgettes), grated
- [ ] 125 g (4 oz) canned corn kernels, drained
- [ ] 3 tablespoons chopped fresh basil
- [ ] freshly ground black pepper
- [ ] 100 g ($3^1/_2$ oz) grated tasty cheese

COCONUT CREAM
- [ ] 125 mL (4 fl oz) coconut cream
- [ ] 1 tablespoon lemon juice
- [ ] 2 tablespoons chopped fresh mint

1 Drain mung beans and place in food processor or blender with eggs and process until smooth. Place mung bean mixture in a large mixing bowl.

2 Heat 1 tablespoon oil in a frypan and cook onion gently for 3-4 minutes. Add potatoes, carrots and zucchini (courgettes) and cook, stirring for 5 minutes or until vegetables soften. Remove from pan and pat dry with absorbent kitchen paper. Combine cooked vegetables, bean mixture, corn kernels and basil. Mix and season to taste with pepper.

2 Heat remaining oil in a large frypan, add vegetable mixture and sprinkle with cheese. Cook over a low heat for 5-8 minutes or until just firm, shaking pan occasionally to ensure that the frittata does not stick. Place pan under a preheated grill for 3 minutes, or until the frittata is browned on the top.

3 To make cream, place coconut cream, lemon juice and mint in a screw-top jar and shake well to combine. Invert frittata onto a plate, cut into wedges and serve with Coconut Cream.

BESAN FLOUR

Besan flour is flour made from chick peas and can be found at Asian specialty food stores.

Plates Villeroy & Boch

STIR-FRIED VEGETABLES WITH EGGS

Often called Egg Foo Yung and traditionally made with prawns, fish or beef, this popular recipe is delicious just made with vegetables.

Serves 2

- ☐ **125 g (4 oz) snow peas (mange tout), trimmed**
- ☐ **185 g (6 oz) fresh asparagus, cut into 5 cm (2 in) pieces**
- ☐ **3 eggs**
- ☐ **1 teaspoon sesame oil**
- ☐ **3 tablespoons water**
- ☐ **1 teaspoon dry sherry**
- ☐ **1 teaspoon soy sauce**
- ☐ **freshly ground black pepper**
- ☐ **1 tablespoon vegetable oil**
- ☐ **3 spring onions (shallots), chopped**

1 Boil, steam or microwave snow peas (mange tout) and asparagus separately until just tender. Drain. Refresh under cold running water. Drain well and set aside.

2 Place eggs, sesame oil, water, sherry and soy sauce in a bowl and whisk lightly to combine. Season to taste with pepper.

3 Heat oil in a wok or frypan, add egg mixture and stir-fry for 1 minute, or until egg just begins to set. Add snow peas (mange tout), asparagus and spring onions (shallots), and stir-fry for 1 minute longer. Serve immediately.

INDIAN EGG CURRY

A delicious egg curry that combines all the tastes of India.

Serves 6

- ☐ **6 hard-boiled eggs, halved lengthways**

SAUCE
- ☐ **1 tablespoon vegetable oil**
- ☐ **1 large onion, finely chopped**
- ☐ **1 clove garlic, crushed**
- ☐ **1 tablespoon finely chopped fresh root ginger**
- ☐ **1 teaspoon ground cumin**
- ☐ **1 teaspoon ground coriander**
- ☐ **$^1/_2$ teaspoon chilli powder**
- ☐ **1 teaspoon ground turmeric**
- ☐ **440 g (14 oz) canned tomatoes, undrained and mashed**
- ☐ **125 mL (4 oz) coconut milk**
- ☐ **freshly ground black pepper**

1 To make sauce, heat oil in a frypan and cook onion, garlic and ginger over a medium heat for 5 minutes or until onion softens. Stir in cumin, coriander, chilli powder and turmeric, and cook for 2 minutes longer.

2 Add tomatoes and coconut milk, bring to the boil, then reduce heat and simmer for 15 minutes or until reduced to a thick sauce. Season to taste with pepper.

3 Place eggs in a shallow baking dish and spoon sauce over. Cover and bake at 180°C (350°F/Gas 4) for 20 minutes or until heated through.

BOILING EGGS

✧ Hard-boiled eggs that are very fresh can be difficult to peel. Try peeling them under cold water.

✧ To prevent a grey-green ring forming around the yolk, take care not to overcook your eggs, and cool cooked eggs immediately in cold running water.

Left: Rainbow Frittata with Coconut Cream, Rice Fritters
Above: Indian Egg Curry, Stir-Fried Vegetables with Eggs

SPINACH PIE

Serve this quick-to-make pie hot or cold. Any leftovers are great to put in school or office lunch boxes.

Serves 8

- [ ] **8 spinach leaves, sticks removed and leaves shredded**
- [ ] **30 g (1 oz) butter**
- [ ] **1 onion, finely chopped**
- [ ] **125 g (4 oz) ricotta cheese**
- [ ] **125 g (4 oz) feta cheese, crumbled**
- [ ] **60 g (2 oz) grated tasty cheese**
- [ ] **3 tablespoons grated Parmesan cheese**
- [ ] **4 eggs, lightly beaten**
- [ ] **1/4 teaspoon ground nutmeg**
- [ ] **freshly ground black pepper**
- [ ] **8 sheets filo pastry**
- [ ] **3 tablespoons olive oil**

1 Boil, steam or microwave spinach until just tender. Drain and cool completely, then squeeze to remove excess liquid. Chop spinach finely and place in a bowl.
2 Melt butter in a frypan and cook onion for 4-5 minutes or until golden. Combine onion, spinach, ricotta, feta, tasty and Parmesan cheeses. Mix together eggs, nutmeg and pepper to taste, then fold through spinach mixture.
3 Layer 4 sheets of pastry together, brushing between each sheet with oil. Repeat with remaining sheets. Line a deep lightly greased ovenproof dish with a pastry layer. Trim edges with scissors about 2.5 cm (1 in) from the edge of dish. Spoon in spinach filling, then fold remaining pastry layer in half and place on top of spinach filling. Gently fold edges of pastry together, brush top with oil and bake at 200°C (400°F/Gas 6) for 40-45 minutes or until golden and crisp.

VEGETABLE TIPS

✧ Wash vegetables before preparing, but do not soak.
✧ Soaking tends to draw out the valuable water soluble vitamins resulting in vegetables with a lower nutrient content.
✧ As with every rule there are always exceptions and it may be necessary to soak very dirty vegetables to remove dirt and creepy crawlies. In these cases always keep soaking times to a minimum.
✧ Many of the precious vitamins and minerals found in vegetables are stored just under their skin. Only peel vegetables if absolutely necessary.

ORIENTAL TOSS

This is delicious when served on a bed of fine egg noodles.

Serves 6

- [ ] **3 celery stalks, cut into thin strips**
- [ ] **3 carrots, cut into thin strips**
- [ ] **3 zucchini (courgettes), cut into thin strips**
- [ ] **2 large leeks, cut into thin strips**
- [ ] **1 parsnip, cut into thin strips**
- [ ] **125 g (4 oz) bean sprouts**
- [ ] **2 tablespoons vegetable oil**
- [ ] **1 onion, sliced**
- [ ] **1 tablespoon cornflour, blended with 2 tablespoons water**
- [ ] **3 tablespoons sesame seeds, toasted**

MARINADE
- [ ] **1 teaspoon grated fresh root ginger**
- [ ] **2 cloves garlic, crushed**
- [ ] **60 mL (2 fl oz) dry sherry**
- [ ] **125 mL (4 fl oz) teriyaki sauce**
- [ ] **4 tablespoons honey, warmed**

1 To make marinade, combine ginger, garlic, sherry, teriyaki sauce and honey in a large bowl and mix well. Add celery, carrots, zucchini (courgettes), leeks, parsnip and bean sprouts, and toss to combine. Cover and refrigerate for 1 hour.
2 Heat oil in a wok or frypan and cook onion for 4-5 minutes or until golden. Drain vegetables and reserve half of marinade. Add vegetables to wok and stir-fry for 5 minutes.
3 Combine reserved marinade and cornflour mixture and stir into vegetables. Bring to the boil, reduce heat and simmer until sauce thickens slightly. Sprinkle with sesame seeds and serve.

FETTUCCINE WITH WINE AND MUSHROOMS

The perfect way to serve fettuccine – with a magnificent creamy sauce laden with button mushrooms.

Serves 6

- [ ] **600 g (1 1/4 lb) fettuccine**
- [ ] **1 tablespoon olive oil**

MUSHROOM SAUCE
- [ ] **1 tablespoon olive oil**
- [ ] **1 large onion, sliced**
- [ ] **2 cloves garlic, crushed**
- [ ] **500 g (1 lb) button mushrooms, sliced**
- [ ] **15 g (1/2 oz) butter**
- [ ] **1 tablespoon plain flour**
- [ ] **60 mL (2 fl oz) white wine**
- [ ] **250 mL (8 fl oz) vegetable stock**
- [ ] **125 mL (4 fl oz) cream (single)**
- [ ] **2 tablespoons chopped fresh basil**
- [ ] **freshly ground black pepper**
- [ ] **2 tablespoons grated Parmesan cheese**
- [ ] **2 tablespoons finely snipped fresh chives**

1 Cook fettuccine in boiling water following packet instructions. Drain and toss in oil. Set aside and keep warm.
2 To make sauce, heat the oil in a saucepan and cook onion and garlic over a gentle heat for 10 minutes or until onion is golden. Stir in the mushrooms and cook for 2 minutes longer. Remove from pan, drain on absorbent kitchen paper and set aside.
3 Melt butter in a clean saucepan, then mix in flour and cook for 2 minutes. Remove from heat and gradually stir in the wine and stock. Cook over a medium heat, stirring constantly until sauce boils and thickens. Whisk in cream and stir in mushroom mixture and basil. Season to taste with pepper and cook gently until heated through.
4 To serve, spoon sauce over hot fettuccine and top with Parmesan cheese and chives.

Spinach Pie, Oriental Toss, Fettuccine with Wine and Mushrooms

Win both ways, cooking with nuts, grains, pulses and vegetables: firstly for your wallet, as these dietary staples are remarkably economical; secondly for your health, as there are few foods more nutritious.

EASY A TO Z
nutrition know how

LEGUMES

Adzuki beans. Small reddish-brown beans with a cream-coloured seam. Their creamy texture is particularly popular in Japan and China where they are used, boiled, mashed and sweetened, in cakes and desserts. They can also be used in soups, pates and savoury dishes.
Preparation and cooking: Cover beans with cold water and soak for 2-2^1/$_2$ hours. To cook: drain, cover with water, then boil gently for 1^1/$_2$-2 hours.
Nutrition: High fibre, low fat. Fair source of protein and iron.
100 grams raw = 560 kilojoules (130 Calories)

Black beans. Small, almost round black beans with a white seam. Popular in the West Indies and in Chinese cuisine. They are a sweet-tasting bean that can also be used in soups, salads and savoury dishes.

Preparation and cooking: Standard preparation. To cook: drain, cover with water, then boil gently for 30-60 minutes.
Nutrition: High fibre, low fat. Good source of protein, iron, potassium and thiamin. Fair source of calcium.
100 grams raw = 1420 kilojoules (340 Calories)

Black-eyed beans. Small, creamy white, kidney-shaped beans with a black eye also known as black-eyed peas. Brought to Europe and America by slave traders in the 17th century, they are now used widely in soups, casseroles and pates.
Preparation and cooking: Standard preparation. To cook: drain, cover with water, then boil gently for about 1 hour.
Nutrition: Excellent source of thiamin and fibre. Low in fat. Good source of protein, iron and potassium.
100 grams raw = 1440 kilojoules (345 Calories)

Borlotti beans. Large, plump, brown, kidney-shaped beans with burgundy markings, also known as Cranberry beans. Popular in Italian cuisine.
Preparation and cooking: Standard preparation, or soak. To cook: drain, cover with water, then boil for 1^1/$_2$-2 hours.
Nutrition: Excellent source of thiamin. High in fibre, low in fat. Good source of protein, iron and potassium. Supplies some calcium.
100 grams raw = 1460 kilojoules (350 Calories)

Broad beans. Flat beans native to North Africa ranging in colour from olive green to brown/cream. Initially cultivated by the ancient Egyptians and Greeks. They are known in Europe as Fava beans and are mostly eaten dried. Broad beans are also eaten fresh.
Preparation and cooking: Standard preparation. To cook: drain, cover with water, then boil gently for about 2^1/$_2$ hours.
Nutrition: Low fat. Good source of vitamin C. Fair source of fibre.
100 grams raw = 300 kilojoules (70 Calories)

Butter beans. Native to South America, these large plump, white beans are similar in shape to broad beans. Available fresh, dried, canned and frozen.
Preparation and cooking: Standard preparation; if you are going to puree them you will also need to soak the beans. If serving whole, they can just be cooked. To cook: drain, cover with water, then boil gently for about 2 hours.
Nutrition: Low fat. Good source of protein, iron, dietary fibre, potassium pyridoxine and thiamin. Supplies some calcium.
100 grams raw = 1160 kilojoules (280 Calories)

Cannelli beans. White kidney beans with square ends. Popular in Italian cuisine. Delicious in soups or salads or in place of haricot beans to make baked beans.
Preparation and cooking: Standard preparation. To cook: drain, cover with water, then boil gently for 1 1/2 hours.
Nutrition: Low fat. Good source of thiamin, protein, iron and fibre. Fair source of calcium.
100 grams raw = 1420 kilojoules (340 Calories)

Chick peas. Available as white Garbanzo or small, brown, Desi Chick peas. Both are round and rough textured with a pointed break at one end. Crunchy and nutty flavour. Popular in Middle Eastern cooking where they are combined with tahini, lemon and garlic to make hummus. In Israel they are used to make a version of felafel. In Greece, roasted chick peas are served with drinks.
Preparation and cooking: Standard preparation. To cook: drain, cover with water, then boil gently for about 1 1/2 hours. If you require softened peas, you will also need to soak them.
Nutrition: High fibre, low fat. Good source of protein, iron and thiamin.
100 grams raw = 1500 kilojoules (360 Calories)

Haricot/Navy beans. Small white oval beans. The term haricot derives from medieval times when dried beans were used chiefly in a pot containing a haricot of meat. Probably best known for their use in commercial baked beans, they were commonly served to the US navy, hence the alternate name. These beans are also delicious in casseroles.
Preparation and cooking: Standard preparation. To cook: drain, cover with water, then boil gently for 1 1/2 hours.
Nutrition: High fibre, low fat. Good source of protein, iron, thiamin and potassium. Fair source of calcium and riboflavin.
100 grams raw = 1150 kilojoules (275 Calories)

Lentils. Popular in European and Indian cuisine, lentils are available in brown, green, orange, yellow and black. They are lens-shaped and may be bought whole or split. Used in soups and casseroles, they are also the main ingredient of the well-known Indian dip, dahl.

Preparation and cooking: No preparation required. To cook: cover with water, then boil. Red lentils will take about 30 minutes and green lentils 1-1 1/2 hours.
Nutrition: High fibre, low fat. Good source of protein, iron, potassium pyridoxine, thiamin and riboflavin.
100 grams raw = 1370 kilojoules (330 Calories)

Lima beans. Native to South America, lima beans are flat kidney-shaped beans which can be either small and green or large and white. They have a soft floury texture and are popular in both salads and hot dishes.
Preparation and cooking: Standard preparation. To cook: drain, cover with water, then boil gently for 1-1 1/2 hours.
Nutrition: Low fat. Fair source of vitamin C, protein, dietary fibre and iron.
100 grams raw = 475 kilojoules (115 Calories)

Mung beans. Widely cultivated in India and China, these small olive green beans are available whole, split and skinless. They are commonly used in stews and salads but are best known in their sprouted form as bean sprouts.
Preparation and cooking: No preparation is required. To cook: cover with water and boil gently for 45-60 minutes.
Nutrition: High fibre, low fat. Good source of protein, iron, thiamin, riboflavin and folate. Some potassium and calcium.
100 grams raw = 980 kilojoules (235 Calories)

Pigeon peas. Native to Africa, these small round cream or brown peas are also eaten in India and the Caribbean. They are delicious pureed and added to stews or mixed in salads.

Preparation and cooking: Standard preparation. To cook: drain, cover with water, then cook for 30-60 minutes

Nutrition: Good source of dietary fibre, protein, iron and potassium. Some calcium.

100 grams raw = 1430 kilojoules (340 Calories)

Red kidney beans. Sweet-tasting, red, kidney-shaped beans. Mostly used in soups, stews and salads. Traditionally used in Creole cooking and in the Mexican dish chilli con carne.

Preparation and cooking: Standard preparation. To cook: drain, cover with water, boil rapidly for 10 -15 minutes, then cook for 1-1½ hours.

Nutrition: High fibre. Good source of protein, iron, potassium, thiamin and pyridoxine. Fair source of calcium.

100 grams raw = 1140 kilojoules (275 Calories)

Soya beans. These small, hard, oval, beige beans are extremely versatile. Originally cultivated in China, soya beans are possibly the most nutritious of all beans and are best known for their by-products which include soy sauce, tofu (bean curd), miso (fermented soya beans), and tempeh (fermented bean paste).

Soya beans are also used to make textured vegetable protein (TVP) and soy bean milk.

Preparation and cooking: Standard preparation. To cook: drain, cover with water, then boil gently for 3½-4 hours.

Nutrition: Excellent source of thiamin. Good source of dietary fibre, protein, iron and potassium. Some calcium.

100 grams raw = 1694 kilojoules (405 Calories)

Split peas. Green and yellow peas are available. The green pea is traditionally used in the English pease pudding. The yellow variety is pureed for soup. In Sweden, this soup is traditionally served on a Thursday evening, to commemorate the last supper of the unpopular King Eric XIV who was done in through a dash of arsenic in his split pea soup!

Preparation and cooking: No preparation necessary. To cook: cover with water, then boil gently for 1-1½ hours, without stirring.

Nutrition: High fibre, low fat. Good source of thiamin, protein and iron.

100 grams raw = 1320 kilojoules (315 Calories)

Whole dried peas. One of the tastiest variety of peas. They are used in purees or pasties, pea soup, pease pudding, or as a fresh pea substitute.

Preparation and cooking: Soak overnight with a pinch of bicarbonate soda. To cook: drain, cover with water, then boil gently for 1 hour.

Nutrition: Good source of thiamin, protein, potassium, fibre and iron.

100 grams raw = 1200 kilojoules (285 Calories)

NUTS

Almonds. Native to the Eastern Mediterranean regions, almonds are the kernels of the fruit of the almond tree. These nuts feature widely in cooking and are used in both sweet and savoury dishes. The nut is encased in a light brown pitted shell and is a long, flat, oval, creamy-coloured nut.

Nutrition: Excellent source of vitamin E. Good source of fibre and riboflavin. Some iron, protein and potassium.

100 grams = 2335 kilojoules (558 Calories)

Fats: 68% mono-unsaturated, 22% polyunsaturated, 10% saturated

Brazil nuts. A creamy-coloured nut with a dark brown skin encased in an angular dull brown grey-coloured shell. Brazil nuts can be used in both sweet and savoury dishes.

Nutrition: Good source of vitamin E and thiamin. Useful source of protein, iron and dietary fibre.

100 grams = 2545 kilojoules (608 Calories)

Fats: 36% mono-unsaturated, 38% polyunsaturated, 26% saturated

Cashew nuts. Kidney-shaped nuts native to Brazil and the West Indies. These nuts were brought to the rest of the world by Portuguese explorers. Cashews are used widely in sweet and savoury dishes. In Brazil they are also used

for making wine and for the production of anacard, the famous cashew nut vinegar.
Nutrition: Useful source of protein, iron and folic acid. Some dietary fibre.
100 g = 2400 kilojoules (575 Calories).
Fats: 62% mono-saturated, 18% polyunsaturated, 20% saturated

Chestnuts. Large, round, greyish-white nuts with a point at one end, encased in a soft reddish brown shell. Often used in desserts, pates and stuffings. In Italy, chestnuts are stewed in wine, while in France braised or pureed nuts provide the traditional garnish for poultry.
Nutrition: Low in fat. Some B vitamins, potassium and dietary fibre.
100 grams = 1025 kilojoules (245 Calories)
Fats: Negligible

Coconuts. The coconut tree is native to Malaya. The white flesh and milk of the coconut is encased in a rough brown husk which is surrounded by a green pod. Supplying a huge amount of products such as milk, butter, cream, oil and copha, coconut is extremely versatile and is used widely in both sweet and savoury cooking.
Nutrition: Good source of fibre, small quantities of other vitamins and minerals.
100 grams fresh = 1445 kilojoules (345 Calories) Fats: 94% saturated, 5% mono-unsaturated, 1% polyunsaturated

Hazelnuts. Small, round, light brown nuts with a pointed end, encased in a hard brown shell. Hazelnuts are native to North America, South East Europe and Asia. Hazelnuts can be used in desserts, stuffings and as a spread.
Nutrition: Rich in vitamin E. Useful amounts of thiamin, pyridoxine and folic acid.
100 grams = 1570 kilojoules (375 Calories)
Fats: 82% mono-unsaturated, 10% polyunsaturated, 8% saturated

Macadamia nuts. Native to Australia, these hard, smooth, brownish, spherical nuts have a creamy, bitter sweet flavour. Macadamia nuts can be used in both sweet and savoury dishes.
Nutrition: Useful source of thiamin. Small amounts of fibre.
100 grams = 3005 kilojoules (718 Calories)
Fats: 82% mono-unsaturated, 2% poly-unsaturated, 16% saturated

Peanuts. Although the most popular of all nuts, peanuts are not a true nut but the pods of a leguminous plant native to South America. Two peanut kernels are encased in each soft brown shell. Peanuts are used predominantly as a cocktail snack, in peanut butter and peanut oil. They are widely

used in savoury dishes and are a favourite on top of ice cream.
Nutrition: Good source of vitamin E, niacin, thiamin and folic acid. Useful source of protein, potassium, pyridoxine and dietary fibre.
100 grams = 2365 kilojoules (565 Calories)
Fats: 52% mono-unsaturated, 33% polyunsaturated, 15% saturated

Pecans. Long, flat, ridged oval-shaped nuts encased in a brittle reddish-brown shell. Native to the southern states of America, they were used widely by Indian tribes, hence their Indian name. Popular in the dessert pecan pie, pecans can also be used in savoury dishes and stuffings.
Nutrition: Useful source of thiamin. Some protein and dietary fibre.
100 grams = 2760 kilojoules (660 Calories)
Fats: 66% mono-unsaturated, 26% polyunsaturated, 8% saturated

Pine nuts. Small, soft, creamy coloured kernels from the cones of a specific pine tree native to Europe, Mexico and southwest America. Pine nuts are classically found in Mediterranean cooking where they are used to make pesto sauce or to stuff vegetables.
Nutrition: Good source of iron, vitamin E and thiamin. Useful source of protein and dietary fibre.
100 grams = 2155 kilojoules (515 Calories)
Fats: 40% mono-unsaturated, 44% polyunsaturated, 16% saturated

Pistachio nuts. Exquisite, pale green nuts with half open shells. Native to the Middle East, they are used in both sweet and savoury dishes. The best Turkish delight and nougat contains pistachio nuts.

Nutrition: Useful source of thiamin, iron and potassium. Small quantities of other vitamins, minerals and dietary fibre.
100 grams = 2415 kilojoules (577 Calories)
Fats: 71% mono-unsaturated, 16% polyunsaturated, 13% saturated

Walnuts. Fruit of the walnut tree, these nuts are thought to have originated from ancient Persia or China. A creamy brown shell encases the kernel which is in two distinct halves. Walnuts are used extensively in sweet and savoury cooking. Walnut oil makes exquisite salad dressing.

Nutrition: Useful source of pyridoxine, thiamin and folic acid. Some protein and dietary fibre.
100 grams = 2165 kilojoules (586 Calories)
Fats: 24% mono-unsaturated, 66% polyunsaturated, 9% saturated

SEEDS

Poppy seeds. Very small, round, black seeds with a distinctive warm dusty flavour native to the northeast Mediterranean region. Although related to the opium poppy, they lack narcotic properties. Generally used on top of breads and crackers or in the traditional poppy seed cake.

Nutrition: As amounts consumed are usually small, nutritional value is insignificant.
100 grams = 65 kilojoules (16 Calories)

Pumpkin seeds. A dull green kernel enclosed in a flat creamy-white shell. Generally eaten as a snack or 'health' food.

Nutrition: Good source of iron and vitamin E. Provide useful amounts of protein, potassium, thiamin and riboflavin if eaten in large quantities.
100 grams = 2265 kilojoules (540 Calories)
Fats: 33% mono-unsaturated, 48% polyunsaturated, 20% saturated

Sesame seeds. Small, flat, cream-coloured seeds from the sesame plant. Originally from Turkey, these seeds have a nutty taste and are probably the most familiar topping on bread. Sesame seeds are used to make the spread tahini which is a component of hummus. They are also used to make the sweet halva.

Nutrition: In the quantities usually consumed they provide small amounts of iron and vitamin E.
100 grams = 2460 kilojoules (586 Calories)
Fats: 40% mono-unsaturated, 46% polyunsaturated, 15% saturated

Sunflower seeds. Medium, flat, oval beige kernels encased in a fawn and black striped shell, native to North America. Generally used as a topping for breads, health food cakes or biscuits. Also used to make safflower oil and margarine.

Nutrition: Good source of iron and vitamin E. Provides useful amounts of protein and niacin. Some thiamin, riboflavin and dietary fibre.
100 grams = 2385 kilojoules (570 Calories)
Fats: 20% mono-unsaturated, 69% polyunsaturated, 11% saturated

GRAINS

Barley. In ancient times, barley was used to make bread. Nowadays, it is more often used as a thickening agent. Barley has a pleasant nutty taste and can be eaten as pot or Scotch barley, pearl barley or barley meal. Preparation and cooking vary according to recipe.

Nutrition: Low fat, high in fibre, carbohydrate, iron, thiamin and niacin.

Buckwheat. Not actually a wheat but a member of the rhubarb family. Used to make Russian kasha, blini and Japanese noodles called soba. Preparation and cooking depend on the recipe.

Nutrition: Low fat, high in fibre, carbohydrate, thiamin, niacin and riboflavin.

Corn. Once the generic term for all grains, corn is a versatile grain that yields many useful products. Preparation and cooking vary according to recipe.

Corn meal: Corn meal is used in johnnycakes, hush puppies, and corn bread in the United States. In Italy, it is used to make a type of porridge called polenta. Corn meal is also used to make tortillas.

Cornflour/cornstarch: The white heart of the corn kernel ground into a powder. It is generally used as a thickening agent for soups and stews.

Nutrition: Low fat, high in fibre, carbohydrate, protein, iron, niacin and thiamin.

Millet and Sorghum. Closely related to each other, their greatest characteristic is that they swell enormously. Both have a pleasant nutty taste and are best cooked and eaten like rice. In India, millet is combined with black beans to make pancakes called ragi doas. Preparation and cooking depend on the recipe.

Nutrition: Low in fat, high in carbohydrate, niacin and thiamin. Some iron.

Oats. Among the most nutritious of all cereals, oats are best known for their use in the Scottish breakfast cereal porridge or oatmeal. Oatmeal comes in three grades of varying coarseness. Medium grade is traditionally used to make porridge, while fine grade is used for baking oatcakes, biscuits and scones. Preparation and cooking depend on the recipe.

Nutrition: High in fibre, carbohydrate, thiamin, folate and vitamin E.

Rice. At least one-third of mankind eats rice as a staple food. There are many varieties and no preparation is required. Cooking varies according to the variety of rice and recipe.

Short-grain rice: The most popular all-purpose rice, particularly suited to dishes where grains need to cling together.

Long-grain rice: Known for its fluffy texture, long-grain rice is good for pilafs, salads and stuffings.

Brown rice: The natural unpolished rice that has a distinctive nutty taste.

Basmati rice: Grown in Bangladesh and Pakistan, this rice is a delicious, aromatic rice ideal for highly spiced Indian dishes.

Piemontese or Arborio rice: Italian rices that are ideal for absorbing a great deal of liquid. Generally used for risotto, paella or jambalaya.

Wild rice: Although related to the rice family, wild rice is actually a seed from an aquatic grass which grows in North America. It has an appealing distinctive nutty flavour. It is quite expensive, and is used more commonly in gourmet cooking.

Ground rice and rice flour: Mostly used for desserts and cakes, or as a thickener.

Nutrition: Low fat, high in fibre, carbohydrate, thiamin, niacin and folate.

Rye. A strong-flavoured grain commonly used in Scandinavia, Russia and Germany. Rye is used to make Pumpernickel and black bread, as well as many crispbreads. It is also the basis of the alcoholic drinks, whisky, gin and beer. Preparation and cooking depend on the recipe.

Nutrition: Low fat, high in fibre, thiamin, riboflavin, pyridoxine and folate.

Wheat. Wheat is available in various forms. Preparation and cooking vary according to variety and recipe.

Wholewheat grain: Can be eaten in the same way as rice or as a type of porridge called 'frumenty'.

Cracked or kibbled wheat: Wholewheat grain which has been cracked between rollers and is eaten in the same way as the wholewheat grain.

Burghul or bulgur: Cracked wheat that has been hulled and parboiled, giving the wheat a lighter texture and making it easier to cook. Used in the Lebanese salad tabbouleh.

Bran: The papery thin layer of the wheat grain. Bran is an excellent source of dietary fibre.

Wheatgerm: The heart of the wheat grain. Wheat germ may be extracted from the wheat grain to improve its keeping qualities. Wheat germ is often eaten as a topping on cereal.

Semolina: Semolina is the floury part of the wheat grain which is left over when the bran and wheat germ are removed. Semolina is used for breakfast cereal or desserts. Flour-coated semolina is used to make couscous, a traditional North African dish.

Plain wholemeal flour: Wholemeal flour is the flour made from the wholewheat grain.

Nutrition: Low fat, high in fibre and carbohydrate. Good source of B vitamins and iron.

Changing your eating habits requires commitment – easy once you taste our delicious vegetarian recipes! Don't launch headlong into vegetarianism, or any major change of eating habits, without thinking about your nutritional needs.

VEGETARIAN

essentials

Changing to a vegetarian diet
✧ Use the following tips as a guideline if you are changing to a vegetarian diet.
✧ Change to a vegetarian diet gradually.
✧ Start by having one vegetarian meal each week and build up slowly.
✧ Don't commence a strict vegetarian diet overnight. The body and palate need time to adapt!
✧ Do some reading on nutrition. If you are unsure about anything, you should consult a dietitian.
✧ Do not change your diet radically when pregnant or breastfeeding. Small, gradual change is best. Get some professional advice.
✧ Small children have high nutrition requirements. Diets containing milk products should be followed.

Types of vegetarians
Vegetarians are generally classified according to the degree to which animal products are consumed or avoided.
✧ Total vegetarians, vegans, consume no animal products.
✧ Lacto-ovo vegetarians eat no animal flesh, but include milk products and eggs in their diet.
✧ Lacto vegetarians consume milk products but no eggs.
✧ Semi- or partial vegetarians consume some groups of animal foods but not all; red meat is excluded but white meats such as poultry or fish may be eaten.
✧ Alternative or 'new' vegetarians – who include fruitarians (fruit only) and followers of the Zen macrobiotic diet – are technically vegetarian. Strict versions of these diets fail to provide adequate nutrients to sustain good health. In general, stricter diets have a greater potential for nutritional inadequacy.

WATCH POINTS FOR VEGETARIANS		
DIET	FOODS AVOIDED	NUTRIENTS AT RISK
Partial Vegetarians	Meat and/or poultry, fish	Iron
Lacto-Ovo Vegetarians	Meat, poultry, fish	Iron, zinc
Lacto Vegetarians	Meat, poultry, fish, eggs	Energy, iron, zinc
Vegan Vegetarians	Meat, poultry, fish, eggs, dairy foods	Energy, protein, iron, calcium, zinc, vitamin B12
Alternative Vegetarians	Generally as vegan, or more restrictive	As above plus others, depending on level of restriction

Protein

⬧ Adults require protein on a daily basis to repair and replace existing proteins.

⬧ During certain stages of life – childhood, adolescence and pregnancy – more protein is required as new body tissues are being built.

⬧ Protein requirements are increased during breastfeeding, as protein is lost in the mother's milk.

⬧ Proteins are made up of smaller units called amino acids – these are the building blocks of protein.

⬧ To make protein, the body requires the twenty-two amino acids in the appropriate quantities and proportions.

⬧ The body can manufacture all but eight of the amino acids (nine in infants). These are known as the essential amino acids, as they should be an essential part of the diet.

⬧ Inadequate consumption of essential amino acids slows down the manufacture of new proteins and will result in weight loss and delayed growth.

⬧ Dietary proteins are found in animal products such as meat, poultry, seafood, eggs and dairy products. Plant foods such as legumes, nuts, seeds and cereals also supply protein.

⬧ Animal products such as meat, poultry, seafood, eggs, milk, cheese and yogurt contain more protein than plant foods. These animal proteins are known as complete proteins since they contain the eight essential amino acids in sufficient quantity and proportion to supply the body with what it needs.

⬧ Proteins found in plant foods like grains, nuts, legumes, and seeds are present in smaller amounts and are known as incomplete proteins as they lack at least one of the essential amino acids.

⬧ Eating a combination of incomplete proteins each day, preferably at the same meal, ensures that all the essential amino acids are supplied in the diet to provide your body with what it needs.

⬧ This combining of foods is known as protein complementation.

THE COMPLETE PROTEIN STORY

Grains
bread, rice, pasta
barley, rye, oats

Milk Products
milk, cheese, yogurt

Rolled oats with milk
Pasta or rice with cheese
Rice custard
Cheese on bread or toast
Yogurt with pasta or rice

Legumes
dried peas, beans,
lentils, nuts

Seeds
sesame, sunflower seeds

Nut and seed mixed snack
Hummus
Stir-fry beans and seeds

Grains
bread, rice, pasta
barley, rye oats

Legumes
dried peas, beans, lentils

Corn tortillas and beans
Rice with dried beans, lentils or nuts
Tofu or dahl with rice
Peanut butter or baked beans on bread or toast

THE VEGETARIAN FAMILY

Vegetarian mothers

✧ Pregnancy and breastfeeding will increase the need for a number of nutrients (energy, protein, calcium, iron, zinc, vitamins, A, C, and many of the B vitamins).

✧ Well-balanced vegetarian diets will meet these increased needs.

✧ Achieving adequate weight gain during pregnancy is sometimes difficult for vegetarian women, particularly anyone who was a little underweight before pregnancy.

✧ Increased food intake between meals generally helps, as does an increased intake of dairy foods or soy milk substitutes (these should be calcium and B12 fortified).

✧ Physicians frequently prescribe iron and folate (a form of vitamin B) supplements for pregnant vegetarian women as a precautionary measure.

✧ Use of supplements during pregnancy or breastfeeding is best coordinated by a physician or dietitian.

✧ Excessive use of supplements is not recommended.

✧ Supplements of vitamin B12 are only necessary for some vegan vegetarians.

✧ Well-nourished women who eat a vegetarian diet can breastfeed just as successfully as non-vegetarians.

✧ Since the energy demands of breastfeeding are quite substantial, some women have problems with weight loss.

✧ Adequate energy, protein, calcium, iron and vitamin B12 intake is essential for mothers at this time.

✧ A well-balanced diet which contains milk or a fortified soy drink will optimise nutrient intake.

Vegetarian children

✧ Infants and children who consume a well-planned vegetarian diet which includes dairy products can meet their nutritional requirements and maintain normal growth.

✧ As the vegetarian diet is high in fibre, and therefore of a bulky nature, it is difficult for children to get enough energy and protein – they simply cannot eat enough food! If this occurs, their growth may be delayed.

✧ The vegan diet is generally not recommended for infants and children unless it is supplemented to meet their nutritional needs.

✧ Inadequate intakes of energy, protein, calcium, iron, riboflavin and vitamin B12 have been reported in children on strict vegan diets. This is most probably because of their inability to eat enough.

✧ The risks of inadequate nutrient intake seem to be highest after weaning, as this is the most rapid stage of growth.

Vegetarian teenagers

✧ Inadequate nutrient intakes (energy, protein, calcium, iron, zinc and vitamin A) have also been reported in vegetarian teenagers.

✧ The growth spurt in teenage years increases nutritional needs. The risks are again higher for those who follow vegan diets.

✧ Teenagers live busy lives and it is often difficult for parents to control what teenagers are eating. One way to ensure at least one good meal a day is to make sure that your teenager eats a good healthy breakfast.

✧ Keeping healthy and interesting snacks in the pantry or refrigerator will also help ensure that your teenager gets enough to eat.

GETTING THE BALANCE RIGHT

The following guide will help you get to know your sources of protein, vitamins and minerals.

Protein	Eggs, milk, cheese, yogurt, soy milk, tofu, vegetarian meat analogues (such as nut meat, textured vegetable protein), legumes (such as dried peas, beans and lentils), nuts, bread, rice, pasta, barley and other grains are the major sources of protein in a vegetarian diet.
Vitamin B12	Eggs, milk, cheese, yogurt, fortified soy products (such as fortified soy milk) are the main sources of vitamin B12 in a vegetarian diet. Since bacteria can make vitamin B12 through a fermentation process, fermented foods (perhaps even the fermentation of ingested foods which occurs in the mouth and intestine) are an additional, but less reliable source of vitamin B12 in a vegetarian diet.
Vitamin D	Found in eggs, margarine, butter, cream, milk and milk products, vitamin D can also be made by the body when it is exposed to sunlight.
Riboflavin	Dairy foods (milk, cheese and yogurt), eggs, legumes (dried peas, beans, and lentils), green leafy vegetables (broccoli and spinach), almonds, yeast extracts and fortified breakfast cereals are important sources of riboflavin in any diet.
Calcium	Include milk, cheese, yogurt, calcium-enriched soy products (such as tofu, TVP (textured vegetable protein), soy milks – with these products it is important to read the labels), legumes, dark green leafy vegetables (broccoli, kale), almonds, sesame seeds, tahini (sesame seed paste) in your diet to ensure adequate calcium intake.
Iron	Legumes, green leafy vegetables, breads, grains and cereals – especially fortified breakfast cereals – are the major sources of iron in a vegetarian diet.
Zinc	Wholegrain cereals, rice, legumes (dried peas, beans and lentils) and nuts are the important sources of zinc in a vegetarian diet.

GOOD REASONS TO EAT VEGETARIAN

Less obesity	Studies of vegetarians report that they are more likely to have a desirable body weight when compared with non-vegetarians, possibly due to the high complex carbohydrate/fibre, low fat nature of their diet.
Less diabetes	Late or maturity onset diabetes, which, as the name suggests, mostly occurs in middle or older age groups, is associated with obesity. The lower incidence of obesity in vegetarians reduces their risk of developing diabetes. The vegetarian diet, being high in complex carbohydrate and fibre whilst low in fat, is ideal for both the prevention and management of diabetes.
Less blood pressure	Elevated blood pressure, also known as hypertension, is related to obesity, and in some individuals, to a high salt intake. Since vegetarians tend to be leaner than non-vegetarians, as a group they have a reduced risk of developing high blood pressure. Many vegetarian diets are also reduced in salt intake.
Less heart disease	Vegetarians are found to have a reduced incidence of heart disease. This is not surprising since they have a lower incidence of obesity, high blood pressure, diabetes, high cholesterol and smoking. The low saturated fat and high fibre diet is also considered to be a major benefit.
Less cancer	Death from all types of cancer is lower in vegetarians than in non-vegetarians. The virtual absence of smoking and the high fibre intake of vegetarians is considered to reduce the risk of developing lung and bowel cancer respectively. Large intakes of dark green or yellow vegetables, which supply carotene, is thought to generally protect the body against developing cancer (carotene is converted to vitamin A in the body). Less obesity and a lower fat intake has been proposed as an explanation for the lower incidence of breast cancer in vegetarian women.
Less bowel disease	Constipation, haemorrhoids and diverticular disease are less common in vegetarians. The high fibre content of their diet improves bowel regularity, which subsequently reduces their risk of developing these diseases.
Longevity	The vegetarians' diet lowers their risk of premature death from heart disease, diabetes and cancers, and enhances their quality of life by reducing illnesses associated with these chronic diseases.

WATCHPOINTS FOR VEGETARIANS

Inadequate protein

Although the amount and quality of protein is less in vegetables and grains than in flesh foods, the appropriate combination of plant foods will meet the body's protein needs.

Vitamin B12

Nutritional deficiencies rarely occur in adults as the body stores approximately 1000 times its daily requirement. This store can last for up to five years. In practical terms, deficiency is more often found in infants and children of vegan parents. The pregnant/breastfeeding vegan mother must therefore take care to ensure that her vitamin B12 intake is adequate.

Vitamin D

The body can also manufacture vitamin D, providing that the skin is exposed to some sunlight. Cod liver oil is the richest dietary source of vitamin D and was often used to treat rickets, the disease associated with a deficiency of vitamin D. This deficiency is rare and essentially only occurs in those persons who get no exposure to sunlight.

Fat

While vegetarian diets are generally low in fat, diets which contain excessive amounts of fat, oils and full-cream dairy foods can be high in fat. To reduce fat, choose reduced-fat dairy foods and minimise intake of fats and oils.

Calcium

Dairy foods are the main source of calcium in the Western diet, although dark green leafy vegetables, legumes, nuts and seeds are useful sources of calcium. Vegetarians who include dairy products in their diets satisfy their calcium requirements most readily. Calcium fortified products are recommended for vegans.

Iron

An adequate iron intake is necessary to prevent iron deficiency anaemia, the symptoms of which include, fatigue, shortness of breath and, in severe cases, palpitations. Although iron is found in vegetables, legumes, and cereals, there is generally less than in flesh foods. Iron in plant foods is also less well absorbed. Vitamin C, found in citrus fruits and juices, aids the absorption of iron from plant foods.

Zinc

Although zinc is found in a large variety of plant foods, its availability to the body is questionable. Phytic acid, found in grains, is considered to reduce the absorption of zinc, although the process of bread-making lowers phytates and improves zinc availability from bread and bread products. Zinc is essential for protein and carbohydrate metabolism. Most vegetarian diets are adequate in zinc.

You can't beat the crunch of home-grown sprouts. Many people today are lavish in their praise of both raw foods and living foods. Sprouts are considered to be the perfect combination.

SPROUTING
know how

How to sprout

1   Place one cup of seeds in a wide-mouthed large glass jar and cover with water at room temperature.

2   Cover opening with a piece of loosely woven cloth or a double thickness of cheesecloth and secure with a strong rubber band. Allow seeds to soak overnight; this encourages germination.

3   The next day drain off the water. Rinse the seeds with fresh water and drain again. Lay the jar on its side to allow for circulation of air around the seeds. Place jar in a dark, warm position or cover with a tea-towel.

4   Rinse the seeds thoroughly and drain twice a day until the sprouts form. They must not be allowed to sit in water otherwise they will rot, nor should they ever dry out.

Seeds sprouts

✦   Sprouts are the young shoots of various rapidly germinating seed plants. They are an important source of vitamins, rich in proteins and minerals, but low in kilojoules (calories). They are also delicious and easily digestible making them one of the best fast foods around.

✦   Sprouts are so versatile in the kitchen that they can be used daily. They can be tossed raw in salads; stir-fried at the last moment in Chinese-style dishes; added to omelettes and scrambled eggs; sprinkled on soups and casseroles just before serving; used as a tasty garnish; and they make a wonderful sandwich filler.

✦   Seed sprouting is easy, quick and inexpensive. They require very little space and are perfect for the flat-dweller without a garden. They can be grown at any time of the year.

✦   Packets of seeds and kits are available from many health food shops. Kits with a built-in drainage facility are the easiest to use. However, a large glass jar and a piece of loosely woven cloth (found at home) are just as efficient.

✦   As seeds increase in volume up to ten times, it is important to choose a glass jar big enough to allow for this.

✦   Always buy seeds that are specifically labelled for sprouting as these will be untreated with chemicals.

✦   Store the sprouts in a plastic bag in the refrigerator to prevent drying. They are best eaten as soon as possible, but will remain in good condition for a few days.

✦   Mustard and cress will grow taller than jar-sprouted seeds if, after an overnight soaking, they are placed on a base of wet cotton wool spread across a plate. Water twice a day and harvest with scissors.

✦   Depending on the type of seed and weather, sprouts will be ready within a few days.

✦   Different seeds need different lengths of time to sprout. The best time to eat sprouts is as soon as the first set of tiny green leaves appear.

✦   Some grain seeds can be sprouted in a little soil in shallow seeding trays.

A dinner party is always fun. This one, with your time planned and exciting dishes to prepare, is sure to please the most discerning diner.

THE BUSY
entertainer

THE MENU

Spicy Peanut Soup

❖

Brown Rice and Vegetable Pie
Two-Pea Salad
Curried Beetroot and Apple Salad
Pumpkin and Parsnip Chips

❖

Hazelnut Ripple Ice Cream

❖

Herbal Tea
Coconut and Walnut Barfi

❖

SPICY PEANUT SOUP

Fragrant with Indian spices – a quickly prepared soup that has an exotic flavour.

Serves 6

- ☐ 45 g (1¹/2 oz) polyunsaturated margarine
- ☐ 1 onion, finely chopped
- ☐ 1 clove garlic, crushed
- ☐ 1 teaspoon curry powder
- ☐ 750 mL (1¹/4 pt) vegetable stock
- ☐ 750 mL (1¹/4 pt) milk
- ☐ 1 tablespoon cornflour, blended with 4 tablespoons milk
- ☐ 750 g (1¹/2 lb) roasted peanuts, ground
- ☐ 6 tablespoons thick sour cream

1   Melt margarine in a large saucepan and cook onion, garlic and curry powder for 4-5 minutes, or until onion softens. Add stock, milk and cornflour mixture.
2   Bring to the boil, stirring occasionally, then reduce heat and simmer for 15-20 minutes. Stir peanuts through. To serve, swirl a spoonful of sour cream through each bowl of soup.

❖

PUMPKIN AND PARSNIP CHIPS

Serves 6

- ☐ olive oil for cooking
- ☐ 750 g (1¹/2 lb) pumpkin, peeled, seeded and cut into thick strips
- ☐ 750 g (1¹/2 lb) parsnip, peeled and cut into thick strips
- ☐ 1 tablespoon ground cumin
- ☐ 60 g (2 oz) grated Parmesan cheese

1   Heat oil in a deep saucepan. Cook pumpkin and parsnip for 6 minutes. Drain on absorbent kitchen paper and set aside.
2   Just prior to serving, reheat the oil and cook chips for 3-4 minutes or until golden brown and crisp. Drain on absorbent kitchen paper.
3   Combine cumin and Parmesan cheese and toss chips in mixture to coat well.

❖

TWO-PEA SALAD

Serves 6

- ☐ 500 g (1 lb) frozen peas
- ☐ 155 g (5 oz) snow peas (mange tout), trimmed
- ☐ 1 clove garlic, crushed
- ☐ 2 tablespoons vegetable oil
- ☐ 2 teaspoons lemon juice
- ☐ 1 small onion, thinly sliced

1   Drop frozen peas into a saucepan of boiling water and cook for 3-4 minutes. Add snow peas (mange tout) for the last minute of cooking. Drain and refresh under cold running water.
2   Spoon peas into a salad bowl and season to taste. Combine garlic, oil and lemon juice. Toss through salad and fold through onion.

THE FINAL TOUCH

An attractively folded napkin adds the final touch to a pretty table. This fold known as the fan is popular and easy to do. It works best with a well-starched or heavy paper napkin.

1   Fold the napkin in half lengthways, then starting at one of the short ends fold the napkin backwards and forwards in concertina style folds to halfway along the length.

2   Hold the folds firmly and fold the napkin lengthways down the middle to bring both ends of the concertina together. Keep the folds in position with one hand and fold the unfolded flap of the napkin over and across the diagonal.

3   Turn the excess flap underneath to support and balance the napkin. Let go of the pleats and allow the fan to fall into position.

BROWN RICE AND VEGETABLE PIE

Serves 6

- ☐ 315 g (10 oz) cooked brown rice
- ☐ 250 g (8 oz) grated tasty cheese
- ☐ 4 tablespoons grated Parmesan cheese
- ☐ 2 spring onions (shallots), chopped
- ☐ 2 zucchini (courgettes), grated
- ☐ 1 carrot, grated
- ☐ 155 g (5 oz) canned asparagus cuts, drained
- ☐ 3 tablespoons pine nuts, toasted
- ☐ 3 eggs, lightly beaten
- ☐ 200 g (6^1/2 oz) unflavoured yogurt
- ☐ freshly ground black pepper

1 Combine rice, tasty and Parmesan cheeses, spring onions (shallots), zucchini (courgettes), carrot, asparagus, pine nuts, eggs and yogurt. Season to taste with pepper.
2 Spoon mixture into a deep well-greased springform pan (tin). Bake at 200°C (400°F/Gas 6) for 40 minutes or until firm. Cut into wedges to serve.

❖

CURRIED BEETROOT AND APPLE SALAD

Serves 6

- ☐ 1 bunch watercress
- ☐ 2 green apples, cored and cut into thin slices
- ☐ 1 tablespoon lemon juice
- ☐ 2 large beetroot, cooked, peeled and cut into wedges
- ☐ 2 spring onions (shallots), chopped
- ☐ 60 g (2 oz) pecan nuts

CURRY DRESSING
- ☐ 2 cloves garlic, crushed
- ☐ 1 teaspoon grated root ginger
- ☐ ^{1}/2 teaspoon ground cumin
- ☐ ^{1}/2 teaspoon ground coriander
- ☐ ^{1}/4 teaspoon chilli powder
- ☐ 2 tablespoons lemon juice
- ☐ 4 tablespoons vegetable oil
- ☐ freshly ground black pepper

1 To make dressing, mix garlic, ginger, cumin, coriander and chilli powder to make a paste. Whisk in lemon juice and oil and season to taste with pepper. Place watercress in a serving bowl and pour over half the dressing. Toss to combine.
2 Toss apples in lemon juice. Top watercress with beetroot then apples, spring onions (shallots) and pecans, and pour over remaining dressing.

HAZELNUT RIPPLE ICE CREAM

An ice cream with a wonderful texture that will have you coming back again and again for just one more scoop. Serve it with fresh fruits and grated chocolate.

Serves 6

- ☐ 125 g (4 oz) wholemeal breadcrumbs made from stale bread
- ☐ 125 g (4 oz) brown sugar
- ☐ 60 g (2 oz) roasted hazelnuts, finely chopped
- ☐ 1^1/2 teaspoons ground cinnamon
- ☐ 1 teaspoon ground mixed spice
- ☐ 1 litre (1^3/4 pt) vanilla ice cream, softened slightly

1 Combine breadcrumbs, sugar and hazelnuts. Place on a baking tray (sheet) and roast at 200°C (400°F/Gas 6) for 12-15 minutes, tossing with a spoon occasionally, or until golden and crunchy.
2 Combine breadcrumb mixture, cinnamon and mixed spice. Fold through ice cream. Pour into a foil-lined freezer tray and freeze until firm.

HERBAL TEAS

Herbal teas are available from all health food shops and some supermarkets. There are many varieties to choose from, and they are a soothing alternative to coffee.

❖

COCONUT AND WALNUT BARFI

Makes 25

- ☐ 30 g (1 oz) ghee
- ☐ 250 mL (8 fl oz) coconut milk
- ☐ 315 g (10 oz) coconut
- ☐ 250 g (8 oz) full cream milk powder
- ☐ 125 g (4 oz) caster sugar
- ☐ 1 teaspoon ground cardamom
- ☐ 60 g (2 oz) walnuts, chopped
- ☐ 60 g (2 oz) dried dates, chopped

1 Melt ghee in a small saucepan. Add coconut milk, coconut, milk powder, sugar, cardamom, walnuts and dates and mix well. Cook, stirring, over a medium heat for 2 minutes.
2 Spoon mixture into lightly greased 23 cm (9 in) square cake pan (tin). Smooth the surface, cover and refrigerate overnight. To serve, remove barfi from pan (tin) and cut into squares.

COUNT DOWN

Knowing where to start and how best to use your time are the secrets of a successful dinner party. This time plan will ensure that your dinner party is ready at the time you want and that you can still enjoy it with your guests.

THE DAY BEFORE
✧ Make up the Coconut and Walnut Barfi and refrigerate.
✧ Prepare the Hazelnut Ripple Ice Cream and freeze.
✧ Prepare and cook the vegetables for the Two-Pea Salad, arrange in the salad bowl, cover and refrigerate.
✧ Make the dressings for both the salads and store in screw-top jars.

ON THE DAY
✧ Make Spicy Peanut Soup, cover and store in the refrigerator until required.
✧ Prepare Brown Rice and Vegetable Pie, cover and refrigerate until required.
✧ Prepare ingredients for Curried Beetroot and Apple Salad. Toss apple in lemon juice, cover and set aside. Cover and refrigerate remaining ingredients.
✧ Prepare Pumpkin and Parsnip Chips and cook the first time, drain and set aside.
✧ Set the table.

ONE HOUR BEFORE
✧ Cook Brown Rice and Vegetable Pie.
✧ Warm Spicy Peanut Soup until heated through.
✧ Toss the salads.
✧ Cut and arrange Coconut and Walnut Barfi on a serving platter, cover and refrigerate.
✧ Cook the Pumpkin and Parsnip Chips for the final time.

Clockwise from left: Curried Beetroot and Apple Salad, Hazelnut Ripple Ice Cream, Coconut and Walnut Barfi, Spicy Peanut Soup, Brown Rice and Vegetable Pie wth Two-Pea Salad and Pumpkin and Parsnip Chips

Plates Limoges Glassware Incorporated Anencies

There's something special about putting a concoction into the oven and having it fill the air with delicious scents – while simultaneously filling the room with ravenous admirers.

A BAKER'S
dozen to delight in

❖

WHOLEMEAL CHERRY AND ALMOND BREAD

An eye-catching, tasty bread that can be served while still warm. Great to serve with coffee in place of dessert.

Makes 30 slices

- ☐ **2 eggs**
- ☐ **125 g (4 oz) caster sugar**
- ☐ **155 g (5 oz) whole blanched almonds**
- ☐ **125 g (4 oz) whole red glace cherries**
- ☐ **125 g (4 oz) self-raising flour, sifted**
- ☐ **125 g (4 oz) wholemeal plain flour, sifted**

1   Place eggs and sugar in a bowl and beat with an electric beater for 6 minutes or until mixture is thick and creamy. Stir in almonds, cherries, self-raising and wholemeal flours.
2   Spread mixture into a greased and lined 7 x 26 cm (3 x 10^1/$_2$ in) bar pan (tin). Bake at 180°C (350°F/Gas 4) for 30-35 minutes or until firm and browned. Cool bread in tin for 15 minutes before turning onto a wire rack to cool completely. Wrap in foil and leave overnight.
3   Cut bread into 3 mm (^{1}/$_8$ in) slices using a sharp knife. Place slices on oven trays in single layers and bake at 180°C (350°F/Gas 4) for 10 minutes or until bread is lightly browned

❖

ORANGE AND LIME YOGURT SYRUP CAKE

Serves 10

- ☐ **125 g (4 oz) butter**
- ☐ **1 teaspoon grated lime rind**
- ☐ **3 teaspoons grated orange rind**
- ☐ **220 g (7 oz) caster sugar**
- ☐ **3 eggs**
- ☐ **200 g (6^1/$_2$ oz) self-raising flour, sifted**
- ☐ **125 g (4 oz) unflavoured yogurt**

SYRUP
- ☐ **2 tablespoons lime juice**
- ☐ **3 tablespoons orange juice**
- ☐ **3 tablespoons sugar**

1   Place butter, lime and orange rinds in a large mixing bowl and beat until light and creamy. Add sugar a little at a time, beating well after each addition.
2   Beat in eggs one at a time and mix well. Fold through flour alternately with yogurt. Spoon mixture into a greased 20 cm (8 in) ring pan (tin). Bake at 180°C (350°F/Gas 4) for 30-35 minutes or until cooked. Stand in cake pan (tin) for 5 minutes, then turn out on a wire rack with a tray underneath.
3   To make syrup, place lime juice, orange juice and sugar in a saucepan. Cook over a medium heat, stirring constantly, until sugar dissolves. Bring mixture to the boil without stirring, and boil for 3 minutes. Remove from heat and pour hot syrup over hot cake. Set aside to cool.

COOK'S TIP

If you have an electric knife, it is ideal for cutting this loaf.

Wholemeal Cherry and Almond Bread, Strawberry Tarts, Orange and Lime Yogurt Syrup Cake

QUEEN OF HEARTS

You might like to change the filling and/or topping for the Strawberry Tarts.

Lemon Tarts: Replace strawberry jam with lemon butter. Top with topping and cook as for Strawberry Tarts.

Orange Tarts: Remove rind and pith from 2 oranges and chop orange flesh. Use in place of strawberry jam. Top with topping and cook as for Strawberry Tarts.

Marmalade Tarts: Replace strawberry jam with marmalade. Top with a rolled oats topping. To make rolled oats topping, place 60 g (2 oz) rolled oats, 60 g (2 oz) brown sugar, 60 g (2 oz) wholemeal self-raising flour in a bowl and stir in 90 g (3 oz) polyunsaturated margarine, melted. Sprinkle over tarts and cook as for Strawberry Tarts.

Jam Tarts: To make plain jam tarts, fill the tarts with a jam of your choice and omit topping. Cook as for Strawberry Tarts.

❖

STRAWBERRY TARTS

The wicked jam and moreish topping will make these tarts disappear in no time.

Makes 24

- ☐ **125 g (4 oz) polyunsaturated margarine**
- ☐ **60 g (2 oz) sugar**
- ☐ **1 egg**
- ☐ **2 teaspoons milk**
- ☐ **250 g (8 oz) self-raising flour, sifted**
- ☐ **185 g (6 oz) strawberry jam**

TOPPING
- ☐ **60 g (2 oz) sugar**
- ☐ **60 g (2 oz) desiccated coconut**
- ☐ **1 egg**

1   Place margarine and sugar in a bowl and beat until light and fluffy. Mix in egg and milk, then flour, mixing to form a dough. Turn out onto a lightly floured surface and roll out thinly, cut into rounds using a 7.5 cm (3 in) cutter and place in lightly greased patty pans (tins). Top with a spoonful of jam.

2   To make topping, place sugar, coconut and egg in a bowl and mix well. Place a spoonful of topping on each tart and bake at 200°C (400°F/Gas 6) for 10-15 minutes, or until tops are golden and bases are cooked.

CRUNCHY ALMOND HONEY BARS

Makes 30

- 15 g (^{1}/2 oz) butter
- 185 g (6 oz) honey
- 60 g (2 oz) flaked almonds, toasted
- 4 tablespoons sunflower seeds
- 2 tablespoons sesame seeds
- 60 g (2 oz) desiccated coconut
- 30 g (1 oz) puffed rice cereal

LEMON ICING
- 250 g (8 oz) icing sugar, sifted
- 15 g (^{1}/2 oz) butter
- 2 tablespoons lemon juice
- 1 tablespoon water

1 Combine butter and honey in a saucepan and bring to the boil, stirring gently. Add almonds, sunflower and sesame seeds and boil gently, without stirring, for 3 minutes.

2 Remove from heat. Stir in coconut and cereal. Spread into a foil-lined 25 x 15 cm (10 x 6 in) shallow cake pan (tin) and press down firmly. Refrigerate until set.

3 To make icing, place icing sugar, butter, lemon juice and water in a mixing bowl and beat until smooth.

4 Remove slice from the pan (tin) and spread with icing. Cut into thin slices.

From left: Crunchy Almond Honey Bars, Honey Banana Cake, Chocolate Caramel Slice, Chocolate Potato Cake

CHOCOLATE CARAMEL SLICE

Makes 25

SHORTBREAD BASE
- 100 g (3^1/2 oz) polyunsaturated margarine
- 3 tablespoons sugar
- 60 g (2 oz) cornflour, sifted
- 100 g (3^1/2 oz) plain flour, sifted

CARAMEL FILLING
- 125 g (4 oz) margarine
- 90 g (3 oz) brown sugar
- 2 tablespoons honey
- 400 g (12^1/2 oz) canned condensed milk
- 1 teaspoon vanilla essence

TOPPING
- 200 g (6^1/2 oz) plain (dark) chocolate melted with 30 g (1 oz) copha

1 To make base, place margarine and sugar in a bowl and beat until light and fluffy. Mix in cornflour and flour, turn out onto a lightly floured surface and knead lightly, then press into a greased and lined 28 x 18 cm (11 x 7 in) shallow cake pan (tin). Bake at 180°C (350°F/Gas 4) for 25 minutes or until firm.

2 To make filling, place margarine, sugar and honey in a saucepan and heat, stirring until sugar dissolves. Bring to the boil and simmer for 7 minutes, then add condensed milk and vanilla and beat well. Pour over base and cook at 180°C (350°F/Gas 4) for 20 minutes. Allow to cool completely.

3 Spread topping over filling and set aside to firm. Cut into squares to serve.

CHOCOLATE POTATO CAKE

Serves 10

- ☐ 125 g (4 oz) butter
- ☐ 155 g (5 oz) caster sugar
- ☐ 1 large potato, cooked and mashed
- ☐ 60 g (2 oz) plain (dark) chocolate, melted
- ☐ 3 tablespoons cocoa powder, sifted
- ☐ 2 eggs
- ☐ 1 tablespoon lemon juice
- ☐ 185 g (6 oz) self-raising flour, sifted with 1/2 teaspoon ground (grated) nutmeg
- ☐ 60 g (2 oz) walnuts, chopped
- ☐ 3 tablespoons milk

ICING
- ☐ 155 g (5 oz) plain (dark) chocolate, melted
- ☐ 250 g (8 oz) thick sour cream

1 Place butter in a large mixing bowl and beat until light and creamy. Add sugar a little at a time, beating well after each addition. Beat in potato, chocolate, cocoa powder and eggs one at a time. Stir in lemon juice.

2 Combine flour mixture and walnuts. Fold lightly through butter mixture alternately with milk. Spoon mixture into a greased and lined 23 cm (9 in) round cake pan (tin). Bake at 180°C (350°F/Gas 4) for 35-40 minutes, or until cooked in the centre when tested with a skewer. Stand in pan (tin) for 5 minutes before turning out on a wire rack to cool.

3 To make icing, place chocolate and sour cream in a mixing bowl and beat until combined. Spread over cold cake.

HONEY BANANA CAKE

Serves 12

- ☐ 155 g (5 oz) wholemeal self-raising flour
- ☐ 125 g (4 oz) self-raising flour
- ☐ 1 teaspoon bicarbonate of soda
- ☐ 1 teaspoon ground (grated) nutmeg
- ☐ 185 g (6 oz) raw sugar
- ☐ 2 tablespoons honey, warmed
- ☐ 4 eggs, lightly beaten
- ☐ 5 bananas, mashed
- ☐ 250 mL (8 fl oz) vegetable oil

HONEY CHEESE TOPPING
- ☐ 125 g (4 oz) cream cheese
- ☐ 2 tablespoons honey
- ☐ ground (grated) nutmeg

1 Sift wholemeal and self-raising flours, bicarbonate of soda and nutmeg into a large mixing bowl. Stir in sugar, honey, eggs, bananas and oil. Beat lightly until smooth.

2 Pour mixture into a greased and lined 23 cm (9 in) square cake pan (tin). Bake at 160°C (325°F/Gas 3) for 1 hour or until cooked when tested with a skewer. Cool in pan (tin) for 10 minutes before turning out onto a wire rack to cool completely.

3 To make topping, place cream cheese and honey in a bowl and beat until smooth and creamy. Spread over cold cake and sprinkle with nutmeg.

HERB AND CHEESE MUFFINS

Perfect for breakfast, brunch or a light snack, these muffins can be frozen and then reheated when required.

Makes 12-18

- ☐ **250 g (8 oz) self-raising flour, sifted**
- ☐ **2 tablespoons unprocessed bran**
- ☐ **1 teaspoon baking powder**
- ☐ **1 tablespoon caster sugar**
- ☐ **60 g (2 oz) grated tasty cheese**
- ☐ **2 tablespoons mixed chopped fresh herbs, such as parsley, chives or basil**
- ☐ **2 spring onions (shallots), finely chopped**
- ☐ **125 g (4 oz) polyunsaturated margarine, melted**
- ☐ **1 egg, lightly beaten**
- ☐ **250 mL (8 fl oz) milk**

1 Combine flour, bran, baking powder and sugar in a large mixing bowl. Stir in cheese, herbs and spring onions (shallots).
2 Combine margarine, egg and milk. Add to flour mixture and mix to combine.
3 Spoon into greased muffin pans (tins) and bake at 180°C (350°F/Gas 4) for 25-30 minutes or until golden brown.

❖

SWEET POTATO TEA CAKE

This delicious coconut-flavoured sweet potato tea cake keeps well and is ideal lunch box fare.

Serves 10

- ☐ **300 g (9¹/₂ oz) orange-fleshed sweet potato, peeled and grated**
- ☐ **250 g (8 oz) brown sugar**
- ☐ **185 g (6 oz) plain flour, sifted**
- ☐ **¹/₂ teaspoon ground cinnamon**
- ☐ **1 teaspoon ground (grated) nutmeg**
- ☐ **¹/₂ teaspoon vanilla essence**
- ☐ **125 mL (4 fl oz) polyunsaturated vegetable oil**
- ☐ **2 eggs, separated**
- ☐ **1 teaspoon bicarbonate soda blended with 5 tablespoons water**
- ☐ **125 g (4 oz) chopped almonds**
- ☐ **60 g (2 oz) desiccated coconut**
- ☐ **30 g (1 oz) shredded coconut**

1 Place sweet potato and half the sugar in a frypan and cook, stirring frequently, for 4-5 minutes. Remove from heat and set aside.
2 Combine flour, cinnamon, nutmeg and remaining sugar in a large bowl. Make a well in the centre of the dry ingredients and stir in vanilla, oil, egg yolks and bicarbonate of soda mixture. Fold in almonds, desiccated coconut and sweet potato mixture.
3 Beat egg whites until stiff peaks form and fold through cake mixture. Spoon batter into a lightly greased and lined 25 x 15 cm (10 x 6 in) loaf pan (tin). Sprinkle with shredded coconut and bake at 180°C (350°F/Gas 4) for 1¹/₄ hours, or until cooked when tested. Stand 5 minutes before turning out onto a wire rack to cool.

❖

SPICY SWEET POTATO AND RAISIN LOAF

Makes 1 loaf

- ☐ **185 g (6 oz) orange-fleshed sweet potato, peeled and roughly chopped**
- ☐ **125 g (4 oz) self-raising flour**
- ☐ **125 g (4 oz) wholemeal self-raising flour**
- ☐ **¹/₂ teaspoon ground cinnamon**
- ☐ **¹/₂ teaspoon ground root ginger**
- ☐ **¹/₂ teaspoon ground (grated) nutmeg**
- ☐ **125 g (4 oz) polyunsaturated margarine**
- ☐ **125 g (4 oz) raw sugar**
- ☐ **125 g (4 oz) raisins, chopped**
- ☐ **90 mL (3 fl oz) milk**
- ☐ **1 egg, lightly beaten**
- ☐ **2 tablespoons vegetable oil**

1 Boil, steam or microwave sweet potato until tender. Drain and place in a food processor or blender and process until smooth. Set aside to cool.
2 Sift flours, cinnamon, ginger and nutmeg into a large mixing bowl and return husks to bowl. Rub in margarine with fingertips, then stir in sugar and raisins.
3 Combine milk, egg and oil. Add milk mixture and sweet potato to the flour mixture and mix well to combine. Spread mixture into a greased and lined 14 x 21 cm (5¹/₂ x 8¹/₂ in) loaf pan (tin). Bake at 180°C (350°F/Gas 4) for 1 hour, or until cooked when tested with a skewer. Cool loaf in pan (tin) for 15 minutes before turning out onto a wire rack to cool completely.

Herb and Cheese Muffins, Sweet Potato Tea Cake, Spicy Sweet Potato and Raisin Loaf

THE FRESH
outdoors

❖

ROASTED RED PEPPER QUICHES

These wonderful quiches bring together the flavours of summer.

Serves 6

- [ ] **500 g (1 lb) prepared or ready-rolled shortcrust pastry, thawed**
- [ ] **3 tablespoons grated Parmesan cheese**

FILLING
- [ ] **15 g (^{1}/$_2$ oz) polyunsaturated margarine**
- [ ] **1 onion, finely sliced**
- [ ] **1 red pepper, roasted and skin removed**
- [ ] **2 eggs**
- [ ] **185 mL (6 fl oz) cream (single)**
- [ ] **freshly ground black pepper**
- [ ] **2 tomatoes, peeled, seeded and chopped**
- [ ] **1 tablespoon finely chopped fresh basil**

1   Line six lightly greased individual flan dishes with pastry. Trim edges and bake blind (see page 86) for 10 minutes at 200°C (400°F/Gas 6). Remove rice and paper, reduce temperature to 180°C (350°F/Gas 4) and bake for 10-15 minutes or until pastry is lightly browned. Set aside to cool.
2   To make filling, melt margarine in a small frypan and cook onion over a medium heat for 5-6 minutes or until soft. Cut pepper into 1 cm (^{1}/$_2$ in) squares. Place eggs and cream in a bowl and whisk to combine. Season to taste with pepper.
3   Divide onion, tomatoes, basil and pepper between the pastry shells. Spoon over egg mixture and sprinkle with Parmesan cheese. Bake at 180°C (350°F/Gas 4) for 15-20 minutes or until firm.

❖

RICE TERRINE

Serves 6

- [ ] **^{1}/$_2$ small cabbage, separated into leaves and blanched**
- [ ] **60 g (2 oz) wild rice**
- [ ] **200 g (6^1/$_2$ oz) long-grain rice**
- [ ] **30 g (1 oz) polyunsaturated margarine**
- [ ] **2 teaspoons ground cumin**
- [ ] **2 teaspoons garam masala**
- [ ] **4 spring onions (shallots), chopped**
- [ ] **2 stalks celery, finely chopped**
- [ ] **2 eggs, lightly beaten**
- [ ] **100 g (3^1/$_2$ oz) grated tasty cheese**
- [ ] **60 g (2 oz) sultanas**
- [ ] **200 g (6^1/$_2$ oz) canned sweet red peppers, drained and chopped**
- [ ] **freshly ground black pepper**

1   Line a lightly greased 25 x 10 cm (10 x 4 in) ovenproof loaf pan (tin) with cabbage leaves. Allow some of the leaves to overhang the top.
2   Cook wild rice in boiling water for 15 minutes, stir in long-grain rice and cook for 15 minutes longer or until rice is tender. Drain and set aside to cool.
3   Heat margarine in a saucepan and cook cumin, garam masala, spring onions (shallots) and celery for 5 minutes or until celery softens. Remove from heat and set aside.
4   Place rice mixture, celery mixture, eggs, cheese, sultanas and red peppers in a large bowl. Season to taste with pepper and mix well to combine. Press into cabbage-lined pan (tin). Fold cabbage leaves over mixture, or use more cabbage leaves to encase filling. Cover with foil and bake at 200°C (400°F/Gas 6) for 35-40 minutes or until cooked through. Stand for 5 minutes. Turn out and cool completely.

❖

EGGS WITH FRESH HERB DRESSING

An attractive salad plate that is perfect for any outing or quick meal. The dressing will keep for several days in the refrigerator and is also great with potato salad.

Serves 6

- [ ] **lettuce leaves**
- [ ] **6 hard-boiled eggs, peeled and quartered**
- [ ] **12 cherry tomatoes**
- [ ] **1 avocado, stoned, peeled and cut into slices**
- [ ] **24 black olives**

FRESH HERB DRESSING
- [ ] **250 g (8 oz) unflavoured yogurt**
- [ ] **2 tablespoons chopped fresh parsley**
- [ ] **1 tablespoon chopped fresh mint**
- [ ] **1 tablespoon snipped fresh chives**
- [ ] **2 tablespoons apple juice**
- [ ] **freshly ground black pepper**

1   To make dressing, place yogurt, parsley, mint, chives and apple juice in a food processor or blender, and process until dressing is combined and green in colour. Season to taste with pepper.
2   Divide lettuce leaves, eggs, tomatoes, avocado slices and olives between six plates and arrange attractively. To serve, spoon dressing over, or serve separately.

❖

SPICED HONEY CREAM AND FRESH FRUIT

Serves 4

- [ ] **250 mL (8 fl oz) vanilla yogurt**
- [ ] **125 mL (4 fl oz) buttermilk**
- [ ] **125 mL (4 fl oz) thickened cream (double)**
- [ ] **2 tablespoons honey, warmed**
- [ ] **^{1}/$_4$ teaspoon ground cinnamon**
- [ ] **^{1}/$_2$ teaspoon ground (grated) nutmeg**
- [ ] **selection roasted nuts**
- [ ] **selection fresh fruit**

Place yogurt, buttermilk, cream, honey, cinnamon and nutmeg in a food processor or blender and process until smooth. Transfer to a bowl, cover and chill. Serve with nuts and fruits.

Spiced Honey Cream and Fresh Fruit, Rice Terrine, Eggs with Fresh Herb Dressing, Roasted Red Pepper Quiches

Plates Pillivuyt

HERBED HOT DOGS

Serves 6

- ☐ **100 g (3^1/$_2$ oz) peanuts, finely chopped**
- ☐ **100 g (3^1/$_2$ oz) cashew nuts, finely chopped**
- ☐ **100 g (3^1/$_2$ oz) pine nuts, finely chopped**
- ☐ **100 g (3^1/$_2$ oz) sunflower kernels, finely chopped**
- ☐ **1 onion, grated**
- ☐ **1 carrot, grated**
- ☐ **1 small red pepper, finely chopped**
- ☐ **2 teaspoons finely chopped fresh marjoram**
- ☐ **2 teaspoons finely chopped fresh thyme**
- ☐ **2 eggs, lightly beaten**
- ☐ **freshly ground black pepper**
- ☐ **60 g (2 oz) sesame seeds**
- ☐ **vegetable oil for cooking**
- ☐ **6 wholemeal bread rolls**
- ☐ **French mustard or tomato sauce**

1 Place peanuts, cashew nuts, pine nuts, sunflower kernels, onion, carrot, pepper, marjoram, thyme and eggs in a bowl and mix well to combine. Season to taste with pepper. Divide into twelve portions and mould each portion into a sausage shape. Roll in sesame seeds.

2 Heat oil in a frypan and cook sausages for 2 minutes each side or until golden. Serve in a bread roll topped with mustard or sauce.

❖

NUT LOAF

Serves 6

- ☐ **315 g (10 oz) unsalted mixed nuts, finely chopped**
- ☐ **100 g (3^1/$_2$ oz) pine nuts, finely chopped**
- ☐ **1 carrot, grated**
- ☐ **1 stalk celery, finely chopped**
- ☐ **1 onion, finely chopped**
- ☐ **1 tomato, peeled and finely chopped**
- ☐ **2 eggs, lightly beaten**
- ☐ **100 g (3^1/$_2$ oz) wholemeal bread-crumbs made from stale bread**
- ☐ **125 g (4 oz) ricotta cheese**
- ☐ **2 teaspoons chopped fresh rosemary**
- ☐ **125 mL (4 fl oz) tomato sauce**
- ☐ **freshly ground black pepper**

1 Combine mixed nuts, pine nuts, carrot, celery, onion, tomato, eggs, breadcrumbs, ricotta cheese, rosemary and tomato sauce. Season to taste with pepper.

2 Press mixture into a lightly greased 15 x 25 cm (6 x 10 in) loaf pan (tin). Bake at 180°C (350°F/Gas 4) for 45 minutes or until firm. Allow to stand for 5 minutes. Turn out to cool.

❖

SPICED HONEYDEW AND APPLE SOUP

Serves 4

- ☐ **1 honeydew melon, peeled, seeded and cut into chunks**
- ☐ **375 mL (12 fl oz) apple juice**
- ☐ **250 mL (8 fl oz) dry white wine**
- ☐ **2 teaspoons lemon juice**
- ☐ **1 teaspoon finely chopped preserved root ginger**
- ☐ **small melon balls and mint sprigs**

Place melon in a food processor or blender and process until smooth. Add apple juice, wine, lemon juice and ginger and blend to combine. Transfer to a bowl, cover and refrigerate for 2 hours. Stir occasionally. Garnish with melon balls and mint.

❖

MARINATED MUSHROOM SALAD

Serves 6

- ☐ **500 g (1 lb) button mushrooms, wiped and sticks removed**
- ☐ **2 large red peppers, seeded and sliced**
- ☐ **250 g (8 oz) snow peas (mange tout), trimmed**

MARINADE
- ☐ **3 tablespoons white vinegar**
- ☐ **3 tablespoons cider vinegar**
- ☐ **3 tablespoons lemon juice**
- ☐ **4 tablespoons olive oil**
- ☐ **1 small red chilli, finely chopped**
- ☐ **2 tablespoons concentrated tomato paste**
- ☐ **1 tablespoon chopped fresh coriander**
- ☐ **1 tablespoon chopped fresh basil**
- ☐ **2 cloves garlic, crushed**

1 Place mushrooms, peppers and snow peas (mange tout) in a large bowl.

2 To make marinade, place white and cider vinegars, lemon juice, oil, chilli, tomato paste, coriander, basil and garlic in a screw-top jar, shake well to combine. Pour over salad and toss to combine. Cover and refrigerate well before serving.

Herbed Hot Dogs, Nut Loaf, Spiced Honeydew and Apple Soup, Marinated Mushroom Salad

Plates Les Olivades Glasses Accoutrement Tiles Pazotti

INDIAN SWEET POTATO RICE PIE

Serves 4

- ☐ **125 g (4 oz) brown rice, cooked**
- ☐ **1 egg, lightly beaten**

FILLING

- ☐ **500 g (1 lb) sweet potato, peeled and chopped**
- ☐ **1 teaspoon curry paste**
- ☐ **15 g ($^1/_2$ oz) polyunsaturated margarine**
- ☐ **1 teaspoon garam masala**
- ☐ **$^1/_2$ teaspoon ground coriander**
- ☐ **$^1/_2$ teaspoon ground cumin**
- ☐ **250 g (8 oz) mushrooms, chopped**
- ☐ **1 small red pepper, finely chopped**
- ☐ **4 spring onions (shallots), chopped**
- ☐ **2 cloves garlic, crushed**
- ☐ **1 egg, lightly beaten with 1 tablespoon milk**

1 Combine rice and egg and press into the base and up sides of a lightly oiled 23 cm (9 in) pie plate.

2 To make filling, boil, steam or microwave sweet potato until tender. Drain and mash with curry paste. Set aside to cool. Melt margarine in a saucepan and cook garam masala, coriander, cumin, mushrooms, pepper, spring onions (shallots) and garlic for 10 minutes, or until almost all the liquid has evaporated. Remove from heat and set aside to cool. Mix mushroom and egg mixtures into mashed sweet potato.

3 Spoon filling into pie plate and bake at 180°C (350°F/Gas 4) for 25 minutes or until set.

VEGETABLE KEBABS WITH NUTTY AVOCADO SAUCE

Serves 4

- ☐ **2 zucchini (courgettes), cut into 1 cm ($^1/_2$ in) pieces**
- ☐ **16 button mushrooms**
- ☐ **1 red pepper, cut into 2.5 cm (1 in) cubes**
- ☐ **4 canned pineapple slices, each cut into 8 pieces**

GLAZE

- ☐ **3 tablespoons olive oil**
- ☐ **1 tablespoon balsamic vinegar**
- ☐ **1 teaspoon chopped fresh basil**
- ☐ **1 clove garlic, crushed**
- ☐ **1 teaspoon grated lime rind**
- ☐ **freshly ground black pepper**

NUTTY AVOCADO SAUCE

- ☐ **1 small ripe avocado, stoned, peeled and roughly chopped**
- ☐ **3 tablespoons unflavoured yogurt**
- ☐ **1 tablespoon lemon juice**
- ☐ **2 tablespoons finely chopped walnuts**
- ☐ **2 teaspoons cider vinegar**
- ☐ **pinch cayenne pepper**

1 Thread zucchini (courgettes), mushrooms, pepper and pineapple alternately onto eight oiled wooden skewers.

2 To make glaze, place oil, vinegar, basil, garlic, lime rind and pepper to taste in a bowl. Whisk to combine and brush over kebabs. Grill or barbecue kebabs for 8-10 minutes, or until vegetables are tender, then turn and brush with remaining glaze halfway through cooking.

3 To make sauce, place avocado, yogurt, lemon juice, walnuts, vinegar and cayenne in a food processor or blender and process until smooth. Serve with kebabs.

Left: Indian Sweet Potato Rice Pie,
Vegetable Kebabs with Nutty Avocado Sauce
Above: Spicy Pea Parathas (page 62),
Marinated Eggplant (Aubergine) and
Tomato Salad

WHAT SIZE?

What is the difference between cubing, dicing, mincing and slicing?

The following guide will help you understand what is meant by the different terms used in a recipe:

Cube: cut into about 1 cm ($\frac{1}{2}$ in) pieces.

Dice: cut into pieces about half the size of cube.

Mince: cut into very small pieces in a mincer or food processor.

Grate: use either a hand grater or a food processor with a grating attachment.

Slice: can be any size ranging from very thin to thick. You can also slice into rings. Another way to slice is to cut diagonally. This is a good way to prepare vegetables such as carrots, celery and zucchini (courgettes) for stir-frying.

❖

MARINATED EGGPLANT (AUBERGINE) AND TOMATO SALAD

Using basil, garlic and balsamic vinegar, this salad combines the flavours of Italy. Serve as a starter, as part of an antipasto platter or take it on a picnic. It is delicious served with pitta bread and yogurt.

Serves 6

☐ **6 baby eggplants (aubergines), cut lengthways into 1 cm ($\frac{1}{2}$ in) slices**
☐ **olive oil**
☐ **3 tomatoes, peeled and thinly sliced**
☐ **4 tablespoons finely chopped fresh basil**
☐ **freshly ground black pepper**

DRESSING
☐ **3 tablespoons balsamic vinegar**
☐ **1 tablespoon olive oil**
☐ **2 cloves garlic, crushed**

1   Brush each eggplant (aubergine) slice generously with olive oil and cook under a preheated grill for 4-5 minutes each side or until golden and tender.

2   To make dressing, place vinegar, oil and garlic in a screw-top jar. Shake well to combine.

3   Place a layer of warm eggplant (aubergine) slices in a shallow ceramic or glass dish. Top with a layer of tomato slices. Sprinkle with a tablespoon of dressing, a tablespoon of basil and season with pepper. Repeat layers until all eggplant (aubergine) and tomatoes are used. Cover and refrigerate for at least 2 hours.

COOK'S TIP

If the eggplant (aubergine) appears to be drying out during cooking, brush with a little more olive oil. This salad is even better if left to marinate overnight.

Salad Bowl/Mosmania

DRESSING

- ☐ **1 tablespoon olive oil**
- ☐ **1 teaspoon grated lime rind**
- ☐ **2 tablespoons lime juice**
- ☐ **1 teaspoon wholegrain mustard**
- ☐ **1 tablespoon honey**
- ☐ **1 tablespoon chopped fresh basil**

1   Bring vegetable stock to the boil and pour over couscous. Set aside to stand for 10 minutes, then drain.

2   Combine couscous, carrot, pepper, tomato, cucumber and avocado in a bowl.

3   To make dressing, place oil, rind, juice, mustard, honey and basil in a screw-top jar. Shake well to combine. Pour over salad and toss. Just prior to serving sprinkle with almonds.

❖

CRUNCHY HONEY AND DATE SLICE

- ☐ **90 g (3 oz) rolled oats**
- ☐ **60 g (2 oz) plain flour, sifted**
- ☐ **100 g (3¹/₂ oz) desiccated coconut**
- ☐ **45 g (1¹/₂ oz) cornflakes, lightly crushed**
- ☐ **90 g (3 oz) raw sugar**
- ☐ **155 g (5 oz) chopped dried dates**
- ☐ **125 g (4 oz) polyunsaturated margarine**
- ☐ **3 tablespoons honey**

CHOCOLATE ICING

- ☐ **90 g (3 oz) polyunsaturated margarine**
- ☐ **250 g (8 oz) icing sugar, sifted**
- ☐ **1 tablespoon cocoa powder, sifted**
- ☐ **2 tablespoons cream (single)**

❖

SPICY PEA PARATHAS

You may like to serve these with a spicy tomato sauce.

Serves 4

- ☐ **250 g (8 oz) wholemeal flour**
- ☐ **250 g (8 oz) plain white flour**
- ☐ **30 g (1 oz) polyunsaturated margarine**
- ☐ **250 mL (8 fl oz) warm water, approximately**

FILLING

- ☐ **1 large potato, cooked and mashed**
- ☐ **45 g (1¹/₂ oz) split peas, cooked and mashed**
- ☐ **125 g (4 oz) ricotta cheese**
- ☐ **2 teaspoons coriander seeds**
- ☐ **2 teaspoon cumin seeds**
- ☐ **1¹/₂ tablespoons sweet fruit chutney**

1   Sift wholemeal and plain flours into a large bowl. Rub in margarine, make a well in the centre and gradually add enough water to form a soft dough. Knead on a lightly floured surface until smooth.

2   To make filling, place potato, split peas, ricotta cheese, coriander and cumin seeds, and chutney in a bowl. Mix well to combine.

3   Divide dough into eight portions and roll into small flat rounds. Place a spoonful of filling in the centre of each round. Mould dough around filling to enclose.

4   Cook parathas on a lightly greased barbecue plate, or in a frypan, for 4 minutes each side or until golden.

❖

COUSCOUS SALAD

With a tasty dressing that has the added piquancy of lime, this salad would be perfect for your next 'al fresco' meal.

Serves 4

- ☐ **250 mL (8 fl oz) vegetable stock or water**
- ☐ **200 g (6¹/₂ oz) couscous**
- ☐ **1 carrot, thinly sliced**
- ☐ **1 red pepper, chopped**
- ☐ **1 tomato, chopped**
- ☐ **1 small cucumber, cubed**
- ☐ **1 avocado, peeled, stoned and cubed**
- ☐ **30 g (1 oz) flaked almonds, toasted**

COUSCOUS

❖   Couscous is a fine semolina made from wheat that originated in North Africa, however variations on the traditional dish can be found in Sicily, France and even Brazil, where it is cuscuz rather than couscous.

❖   It is readily available in packages, much the same as rice, and is served as an accompaniment to a meal.

❖   The name couscous applies both to the uncooked granules and the finished dish.

❖   Cold couscous is a pleasantly bland background for vegetable salads and is particularly delicious when dressed with tart lemon or lime dressing.

1   Place oats, flour, coconut, cornflakes and sugar in a large bowl. Combine dates, margarine and honey in a saucepan and stir over a low heat until butter melts. Bring to boil and remove from heat. Stir honey mixture into dry ingredients and mix well.

2   Press mixture into a greased and lined 18 x 28 cm (7 x 11 in) shallow cake pan (tin). Bake at 180°C (350°F/Gas 4) for 20-25 minutes or until golden. Cool slice in pan (tin) before turning out.

3   To make icing, beat butter in a small bowl until creamy. Add icing sugar, cocoa powder and cream. Beat until icing is a spreadable consistency. Spread over cold slice, allow to set and then cut slice into fingers.

❖

TANGY APPLE AND APRICOT LOAF

An easily prepared moist loaf that is great for picnics and lunch boxes.

Makes 1 loaf

- ☐ **155 g (5 oz) dried apricots, chopped**
- ☐ **125 g (4 oz) dried apples, chopped**
- ☐ **2 teaspoons grated lemon rind**
- ☐ **2 tablespoons lemon juice**
- ☐ **170 mL ($5^{1}/_{2}$ fl oz) water**
- ☐ **185 g (6 oz) brown sugar**
- ☐ **60 g (2 oz) polyunsaturated margarine**
- ☐ **185 g (6 oz) wholemeal self-raising flour, sifted**
- ☐ **60 g (2 oz) self-raising flour, sifted**

1   Place apricots, apples, lemon rind, lemon juice, water, sugar and margarine into a saucepan. Bring to the boil and simmer for 5 minutes. Remove from heat and set aside to cool for 5 minutes.

2   Stir wholemeal and self-raising flours into fruit mixture. Spread mixture into a greased and lined 14 x 21 cm ($5^{1}/_{2}$ x $8^{1}/_{2}$ in) loaf pan (tin). Bake at 180°C (350°F/ Gas 4) for 1 hour, or until centre is cooked when tested with a skewer. Cool loaf in pan (tin) for 15 minutes before turning out onto a wire rack to cool completely.

Left: Couscous Salad
Right: Tangy Apple and Apricot Loaf,
Crunchy Honey and Date Slice

Plates Accoutrement *Silverware* Whitehill Silver

*'Christmas is coming, the vegies are getting fat.'
Well no, it doesn't sound quite right, but there is no
reason why those who choose not to eat meat should
miss out on sharing the good flavours.*

CHRISTMAS FARE
with traditional flavour

❖

SPICY CHRISTMAS NUTS

These nuts are baked rather than fried.

Serves 10

- [ ] **2 teaspoons ground coriander**
- [ ] **1 teaspoon ground cumin**
- [ ] **1 teaspoon garam masala**
- [ ] **$^1/_2$ teaspoon cayenne pepper**
- [ ] **$^1/_2$ teaspoon ground root ginger**
- [ ] **freshly ground black pepper**
- [ ] **250 g (8 oz) whole almonds, blanched**
- [ ] **125 g (4 oz) unsalted cashew nuts**
- [ ] **125 g (4 oz) walnut halves**
- [ ] **1 egg white, lightly beaten**

1   Combine coriander, cumin, garam masala, cayenne pepper, ginger, and pepper and place in a shallow dish. Place almonds, cashew nuts and walnuts in a bowl. Add egg white and toss to coat nuts. Remove with a slotted spoon, then roll in spice mixture.

2   Place on an oven tray (sheet) and bake at 120°C (250°F/Gas $^1/_2$) for 1 hour or until the nuts are dry. Set aside to cool.

FRESH CHESTNUTS

✧ If fresh chestnuts are available they can be used to make the Spicy Chestnut and Apple Soup.

✧ To prepare chestnuts for use, make a small nick in the flat side of each chestnut. Place in a saucepan and cover with cold water, bring to the boil, then remove pan from heat. Remove chestnuts from water one at a time and cut off the shells and remove the inner skin. When this starts to become difficult, return the pan to the heat and bring back to the boil. Repeat process until all chestnuts are shelled.

❖

SPICY CHESTNUT AND APPLE SOUP

Serves 10

- [ ] **30 g (1 oz) polyunsaturated margarine**
- [ ] **2 large onions, finely chopped**
- [ ] **1 clove garlic, crushed**
- [ ] **2 green apples, peeled, cored and roughly chopped**
- [ ] **$^1/_2$ teaspoon ground coriander**
- [ ] **$^1/_2$ teaspoon ground cumin**
- [ ] **$^1/_2$ teaspoon chilli powder**
- [ ] **440 g (14 oz) canned chestnuts, drained, rinsed and roughly chopped**
- [ ] **1.8 litres (3 pt) vegetable stock**
- [ ] **250 mL (8 fl oz) cream (single)**
- [ ] **2 tablespoons dry sherry (optional)**
- [ ] **freshly ground black pepper**

1   Melt margarine in a large saucepan and cook onions, garlic and apples over a medium heat for 5-6 minutes or until onion softens. Stir in coriander, cumin and chilli powder and cook for 1 minute longer.

2   Add chestnuts and stock to pan, bring to the boil and simmer for 30 minutes. Remove pan from heat and set aside to cool for 15 minutes. Transfer soup to food processor or blender and process until smooth. Return soup to a clean pan, stir in cream and heat gently. Just prior to serving, stir in sherry and season to taste with pepper.

Clockwise from left: Spicy Chestnut and Apple Soup, Christmas Koulibiaca (page 66), Spicy Christmas Nuts, Fruit Mince Flan (page 67), Blue Cheese Flans with Cranberry Sauce (page 66), Watercress and Goats' Cheese Salad (page 67), Three-Rice Salad Wrapped in Leaves (page 66)

Plates Villeroy & Boch Glasses Saywell *Silverware* Whitehill Silver

❖

CHRISTMAS KOULIBIACA

A flavoursome dish. Make the fillings the day before, and scoop the centre from the loaf earlier in the day, leaving just the filling and final baking prior to your dinner.

Serves 10

- ☐ **1 loaf wholegrain bread**

STUFFING LAYER
- ☐ **60 g (2 oz) polyunsaturated margarine**
- ☐ **1 onion, finely chopped**
- ☐ **1/2 teaspoon dried rosemary**
- ☐ **1/2 teaspoon dried thyme**
- ☐ **1/2 teaspoon dried oregano**
- ☐ **breadcrumbs (see method)**
- ☐ **freshly ground black pepper**

TOMATO LAYER
- ☐ **1 tablespoon vegetable oil**
- ☐ **1 large onion, sliced**
- ☐ **1 clove garlic, crushed**
- ☐ **1 small red chilli, seeded and finely chopped**
- ☐ **440 g (14 oz) canned peeled tomatoes, mashed and undrained**
- ☐ **freshly ground black pepper**
- ☐ **1 tablespoon chopped fresh basil**

SPINACH LAYER
- ☐ **500 g (1 lb) spinach, stalks removed and leaves chopped**
- ☐ **250 g (8 oz) ricotta cheese**
- ☐ **1 tablespoon grated Parmesan cheese**
- ☐ **pinch ground (grated) nutmeg**
- ☐ **freshly ground black pepper**

EGGPLANT (AUBERGINE) LAYER
- ☐ **1 small eggplant (aubergine)**
- ☐ **1 tablespoon vegetable oil**
- ☐ **1 large onion, chopped**
- ☐ **30 g (1 oz) polyunsaturated margarine**
- ☐ **60 g (2 oz) button mushrooms, sliced**
- ☐ **freshly ground black pepper**

1   Cut a slice from top of loaf of bread and scoop out centre leaving a shell approximately 1 cm (1/2 in) thick. Reserve breadcrumbs for stuffing. Set loaf and lid aside.
2   To make stuffing, melt margarine in a frypan and cook onion, rosemary, thyme and oregano for 4-5 minutes, or until onion softens. Mix with breadcrumbs and season to taste with pepper. Set aside.
3   To make tomato layer, heat oil in a frypan and cook onion, garlic and chilli for 5 minutes, or until onion softens. Stir in tomatoes and simmer for 30 minutes, or until a very thick tomato sauce forms. Season to taste with pepper and stir in basil. Set aside to cool.

4   To make spinach layer, steam, microwave or pan cook spinach leaves until wilted. Drain and set aside to cool. Using your hands, squeeze as much liquid as possible from spinach and chop. Place spinach, ricotta, Parmesan cheese and nutmeg in a bowl. Mix to combine and season to taste with pepper. Set aside.
5   To make eggplant (aubergine) layer, bake eggplant (aubergine) in oven at 180°C (350°F/Gas 4) for 40 minutes or until tender. Remove from oven and set aside until cool enough to handle. Peel and mash eggplant (aubergine). Heat oil in a frypan and cook onion for 5 minutes or until soft. Remove onion from pan and drain on absorbent kitchen paper. Melt margarine in frypan and cook mushrooms for 3-4 minutes or until just tender. Remove mushrooms and drain on absorbent kitchen paper. Place in a bowl eggplant (aubergine), onions, mushrooms, 2 tablespoons stuffing and pepper to taste. Mix to combine.
6   To assemble koulibiaca, spoon eggplant (aubergine) filling into base of shell and smooth top using a spatula. Spoon over one-third of stuffing, then top with spinach filling and smooth top. Spoon over another one-third of stuffing, then tomato mixture and finally remaining stuffing. Replace lid and bake at 180°C (350°F/Gas 4) for 1 hour or until heated through. If top starts to brown too much during cooking, cover with foil. Serve koulibiaca hot, cut into slices, with Rich Tomato Sauce (see recipe page 85).

❖

BLUE CHEESE FLANS WITH CRANBERRY SAUCE

Serves 10

- ☐ **375 g (12 oz) or ready-rolled puff pastry, thawed**
- ☐ **30 g (1 oz) polyunsaturated margarine**
- ☐ **2 onions, finely sliced**

FILLING
- ☐ **6 eggs**
- ☐ **280 mL (9 fl oz) cream (single)**
- ☐ **280 mL (9 fl oz) milk**
- ☐ **freshly ground black pepper**
- ☐ **185 g (6 oz) blue cheese, crumbled**

CRANBERRY SAUCE
- ☐ **250 g (8 oz) bottled cranberry sauce**
- ☐ **125 mL (4 fl oz) port or red wine**
- ☐ **1/2 teaspoon ground allspice**
- ☐ **2 teaspoons cornflour blended with 4 tablespoons water**

1   Line ten greased 12 cm (5 in) individual flan tins with pastry. Melt margarine in a small frypan and cook onions for 10 minutes or until soft and golden. Divide into ten portions and spread over base of flans.
2   To make filling, place eggs, cream and pepper in a bowl and mix to combine. Stir in cheese, spoon mixture into flans and bake at 200°C (400°F/Gas 6) for 25-30 minutes or until firm and golden.
3   To make sauce, place cranberry sauce, port and allspice in a saucepan, bring to the boil, then reduce heat and simmer for 5 minutes. Stir in cornflour mixture and cook until sauce thickens. Serve with hot or warm flans.

❖

THREE-RICE SALAD WRAPPED IN LEAVES

Serves 10

- ☐ **10 large lettuce leaves, blanched**

RICE SALAD
- ☐ **125 g (4 oz) long-grain wild rice, cooked**
- ☐ **125 g (4 oz) short-grain brown rice, cooked**
- ☐ **125 g (4 oz) white rice, cooked**
- ☐ **2 spring onions (shallots), finely chopped**
- ☐ **1 tablespoon finely snipped fresh chives**
- ☐ **1 tablespoon finely chopped fresh mint**
- ☐ **1 tablespoon finely chopped fresh parsley**
- ☐ **1 green apple, cored and finely chopped**
- ☐ **3 tablespoons slivered almonds, toasted**
- ☐ **freshly ground black pepper**

DRESSING
- ☐ **1 clove garlic, crushed**
- ☐ **2 tablespoons olive oil**
- ☐ **2 tablespoons balsamic vinegar**
- ☐ **1 tablespoon fresh lime juice**

1   To make salad, place wild, brown and white rice, spring onions (shallots), chives, mint, parsley, apple and almonds in a bowl and toss to combine.
2   To make dressing, place garlic, oil, vinegar and lime juice in a screw-top jar and shake well to combine. Pour over salad and season to taste with pepper. Toss to coat all ingredients with dressing.
3   Place a spoonful of salad in centre of each lettuce leaf. Fold leaf around salad to form a parcel.

WATERCRESS AND GOATS' CHEESE SALAD

Serves 6

- [ ] **1 bunch watercress**
- [ ] **1 butter lettuce, washed and leaves separated**
- [ ] **60 g (2 oz) hazelnuts, roughly chopped**

HAZELNUT DRESSING
- [ ] **2 tablespoons hazelnut oil**
- [ ] **4 tablespoons white wine vinegar**
- [ ] **1 teaspoon Dijon-style mustard**
- [ ] **freshly ground black pepper**

CROUTONS
- [ ] **125 g (4 oz) goats' cheese**
- [ ] **1 clove garlic, crushed**
- [ ] **2 tablespoons finely snipped fresh chives**
- [ ] **4 slices wholemeal bread, toasted on one side**

1 To make dressing, place oil, vinegar and mustard in a screw-top jar and shake well to combine. Season to taste with pepper. Combine watercress and lettuce in a bowl and toss with dressing. Arrange salad on six plates. Sprinkle with hazelnuts and set aside.

2 To make croutons, mash cheese, garlic and chives together and spread over untoasted side of bread. Cut bread into 2.5 cm (1 in) cubes and cook under a preheated grill for 5 minutes, or until cheese is melted and golden. Top salad with hot croutons and serve immediately.

❖

FRUIT MINCE FLAN

Mince pies have been associated with Christmas since Tudor times. Originally they were a mixture of minced or shredded meat, dried fruits and spices. By the end of the nineteenth century the meat was omitted and the mince pie as we know it today was born. The modern mince pie makes ideal vegetarian food.

Serves 10

- [ ] **1 egg, lightly beaten with 1 tablespoon water**
- [ ] **60 g (2 oz) icing sugar, sifted**

PASTRY
- [ ] **125 g (4 oz) polyunsaturated margarine**
- [ ] **60 g (2 oz) sugar**
- [ ] **1 egg**
- [ ] **2 teaspoons milk**
- [ ] **250 g (8 oz) self-raising flour**

FILLING
- [ ] **125 mL (4 fl oz) apple juice**
- [ ] **90 g (3 oz) brown sugar**
- [ ] **1 green apple, peeled, cored and roughly chopped**
- [ ] **1 pear, peeled, cored and roughly chopped**
- [ ] **60 g (2 oz) dried apricots, chopped**
- [ ] **125 g (4 oz) currants**
- [ ] **125 g (4 oz) sultanas**
- [ ] **60 g (2 oz) dried figs, chopped**
- [ ] **30 g (1 oz) glace cherries, chopped**
- [ ] **30 g (1 oz) almonds, finely chopped**
- [ ] **30 g (1 oz) hazelnuts, finely chopped**
- [ ] **$1/2$ teaspoon ground (grated) nutmeg**
- [ ] **$1/2$ teaspoon ground cinnamon**
- [ ] **$1/4$ teaspoon ground mixed spice**
- [ ] **1 tablespoon lemon juice**
- [ ] **1 tablespoon orange juice**
- [ ] **1 teaspoon grated lemon rind**
- [ ] **1 teaspoon grated orange rind**
- [ ] **2 tablespoons brandy**

1 To make filling, place apple juice and sugar in a large saucepan and cook over a gentle heat for 4-5 minutes, or until sugar dissolves. Stir in apple, pear, apricots, currants, sultanas, figs, cherries, almonds, hazelnuts, nutmeg, cinnamon, mixed spice, lemon and orange juices, lemon and orange rinds and brandy. Bring slowly to the boil, stirring constantly. Reduce heat, cover and simmer gently, stirring occasionally, for 25-30 minutes, or until fruit mixture is a soft pulp. Remove pan from heat and set aside to cool completely.

2 To make pastry, place margarine and sugar in a bowl and beat until light and fluffy. Mix in egg and milk, then flour, mixing to form a dough. Turn out onto a lightly floured surface. Roll out three-quarters of the pastry to line a lightly greased 25 cm (10 in) flan dish. Trim edges and bake blind at 200°C (400°F/Gas 6) for 10 minutes. Remove blind bake and reduce heat to 180°C (350°F/Gas 4). Bake for 12-15 minutes longer, or until pastry is light golden. Set aside to cool.

3 Spread filling over pastry shell. Roll out remaining pastry and cut into 1 cm ($1/2$ in) strips and arrange in a lattice pattern on top of fruit. Brush pastry with egg mixture and bake at 200°C (400°F/Gas 6) for 15-20 minutes, or until pastry is golden and filling hot. Serve warm or at room temperature. Just prior to serving, sprinkle with icing sugar.

CHRISTMAS SPIRIT

Christmas is a time for entertaining, and these drinks will ensure that any entertaining you do will go off with a real bang.

❖

EGGNOG

Eggnog is a traditional Christmas eve or morning drink. If you wish, you can make it without the rum and brandy. Just increase the amount of cream and milk you use.

Serves 10

- [ ] **5 eggs**
- [ ] **250 mL (8 fl oz) milk**
- [ ] **250 mL (8 fl oz) cream (single)**
- [ ] **250 mL (8 fl oz) dark rum**
- [ ] **250 mL (8 fl oz) brandy**
- [ ] **4 tablespoons caster sugar**
- [ ] **2 teaspoons vanilla essence**
- [ ] **ice cubes**
- [ ] **ground (grated) nutmeg**

Place eggs, milk, cream, rum, brandy, sugar and vanilla essence in a food processor or blender and process to combine. Place ice cubes in glasses and pour over eggnog. Dust with nutmeg and serve.

❖

MULLED WINE

In Saxon times and for many centuries, it was customary to have the wassail bowl steaming throughout the Christmas period. This is the modern day version, and is fun to serve to your guests at this festive time of year.

Serves 10

- [ ] **12 sugar cubes**
- [ ] **strips lemon rind**
- [ ] **strips orange rind**
- [ ] **6 cloves**
- [ ] **1 cinnamon stick**
- [ ] **250 mL (8 fl oz) cold water**
- [ ] **2 bottles red wine**

1 Place sugar cubes, lemon and orange rinds, cloves, cinnamon stick and water in saucepan. Bring to the boil and cook until sugar dissolves.

2 Add wine and bring to just below boiling point. Strain into a warm jug and serve in warmed glasses.

Those interested in following a healthier eating pattern no longer need to turn down the final course. The honeys, berries, nuts and yogurts of this world – all good for you – can be combined into some fabulous treats.

RICH REWARDS
sweet treats

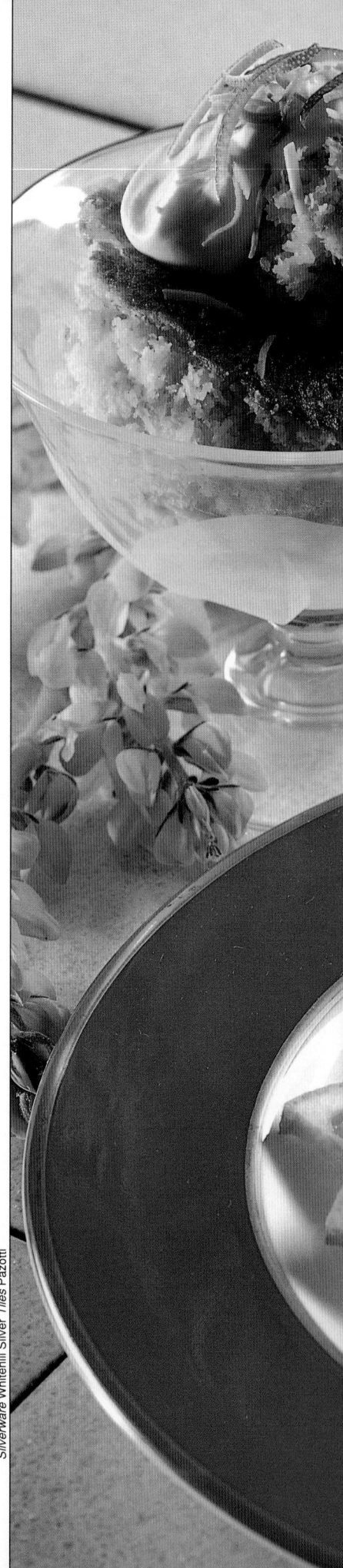

❖

PASSION FRUIT MOUSSE WITH ORANGE SAUCE

Ricotta and reduced-fat cream make this a 'not-so-wicked' dessert for the weight-conscious cook. The Orange Sauce is a perfect alternative to cream.

Serves 6

- ☐ **200 g (6¹/2 oz) ricotta cheese**
- ☐ **125 mL (4 fl oz) reduced-fat cream**
- ☐ **2 tablespoons icing sugar**
- ☐ **1 tablespoon gelatine dissolved in 2 tablespoons hot water**
- ☐ **60 mL (2 fl oz) passion fruit pulp**
- ☐ **3 egg whites**

ORANGE SAUCE
- ☐ **200 mL (6¹/2 fl oz) fresh orange juice, strained**
- ☐ **100 mL (3¹/2 fl oz) clear apple juice**
- ☐ **2 tablespoons sugar**
- ☐ **2 teaspoons arrowroot blended with 2 tablespoons water**

1   Place ricotta, cream and icing sugar in a food processor or blender and process until smooth. Stir in gelatine mixture and passion fruit pulp. Mix well. Whisk egg whites until soft peaks form and then fold into passion fruit mixture. Spoon mixture into six individual (125 mL/4 fl oz capacity) wetted moulds. Refrigerate until set.
2   To make sauce, combine orange juice, apple juice and sugar in a saucepan and cook over a low heat, stirring frequently, until sugar dissolves. Bring to the boil, then reduce heat and simmer for 3 minutes. Stir in arrowroot mixture and cook over a medium heat, stirring frequently, until sauce boils and thickens. Remove from heat and set aside to cool. Refrigerate sauce until well chilled. Turn out moulds and serve with sauce.

❖

STRAWBERRY AND ALMOND TOFU SURPRISE

A wonderfully light summer dessert with a smooth texture. Served in slices with fresh berries and toasted coconut, it makes an extra special finale for a dinner party.

Serves 8

- ☐ **185 g (6 oz) whole almonds, toasted**
- ☐ **2 tablespoons desiccated coconut, toasted**

FILLING
- ☐ **200 g (6¹/2 oz) strawberries, hulled and roughly chopped**
- ☐ **300 g (9¹/2 oz) soft tofu**
- ☐ **125 mL (4 fl oz) coconut milk**
- ☐ **125 g (4 oz) caster sugar**

1   Place almonds and coconut in a food processor or blender and process until evenly chopped. Sprinkle half the nut mixture over the base of a greased and foil-lined 18 cm (7 in) springform pan (tin).
2   To make filling, place strawberries, tofu, coconut milk and sugar in a food processor or blender and process until smooth. Pour mixture carefully over nuts in pan (tin). Sprinkle remaining nut mixture evenly over filling and freeze until firm.

Strawberry and Almond Tofu Surprise, Lime and Coconut Baked Custard, Passion Fruit Mousse with Orange Sauce

Silverware Whitehill Silver Tiles Pazotti

❖

LIME AND COCONUT BAKED CUSTARD

Serves 6

- ☐ **3 eggs**
- ☐ **4 egg yolks**
- ☐ **185 g (6 oz) caster sugar**
- ☐ **375 mL (12 fl oz) coconut milk**
- ☐ **125 mL (4 fl oz) cream (single)**
- ☐ **250 mL (8 fl oz) milk**
- ☐ **375 g (12 oz) desiccated coconut**
- ☐ **2 tablespoons grated lime rind**
- ☐ **ground (grated) nutmeg for dusting**
- ☐ **toasted shredded coconut**
- ☐ **lime rind for garnishing**

1   Beat eggs, egg yolks, and sugar in a bowl until light and fluffy.

2   Combine coconut milk, cream and milk in a saucepan and heat until almost boiling. Remove from heat and set aside to cool slightly. Gradually pour milk mixture into egg mixture and beat until combined. Mix in coconut and lime rind.

3   Pour custard into a buttered 600 mL (1 pt) ovenproof dish. Stand dish in a baking pan (tin) and add enough boiling water to come halfway up the sides of the dish. Bake at 180°C (350°F/Gas 4) for 1 hour or until set.

4   Remove from oven. Dust with nutmeg and decorate with shredded coconut and lime rind. Serve warm.

WHEATY PEACH AND MANGO CRUMBLE

Serves 8

- ☐ **440 g (14 oz) canned mango slices, drained**
- ☐ **440 g (14 oz) canned peach slices, drained**

FILLING
- ☐ **200 g (6¹/₂ oz) peach and mango flavoured yogurt**
- ☐ **2 tablespoons thick sour cream**
- ☐ **2 eggs, separated**
- ☐ **60 g (2 oz) sugar**
- ☐ **2 teaspoons plain flour**

TOPPING
- ☐ **90 g (3 oz) wholemeal plain flour**
- ☐ **2 Weet-Bix (Weet-a-Bix), finely crushed**
- ☐ **2 tablespoons desiccated coconut**
- ☐ **4 tablespoons brown sugar**
- ☐ **1 teaspoon grated lemon rind**
- ☐ **90 g (3 oz) polyunsaturated margarine, melted**

1 Arrange mango and peach slices over the base of a shallow ovenproof dish.

2 To make filling, place yogurt, sour cream, egg yolks, sugar and flour in a bowl and mix well to combine. Beat egg whites until soft peaks form, then fold in yogurt mixture and pour over fruit.

3 To make topping, place flour, Weet-Bix (Weet-a-Bix), coconut, sugar, lemon rind and margarine in a bowl and mix well. Sprinkle evenly over filling and bake at 180°C (350°F/Gas 4) for 30 minutes, or until filling is set and topping browned.

SOUFFLE COLLARS

Cut a piece of greaseproof paper 5 cm (2 in) longer than the circumference of the souffle dish. Fold in half lengthways to give a double thickness. Brush with melted butter and sprinkle with dry breadcrumbs for a savoury souffle, or caster sugar for a sweet souffle. Wrap the collar around the souffle dish. The souffle dish should also be greased and sprinkled with breadcrumbs or sugar – the collar should extend 5 cm (2 in) above the rim of the dish. Tie in place with string.

CARROT AND LIME SOUFFLES

Serves 6

- ☐ **3 carrots, peeled and roughly chopped**
- ☐ **3 eggs**
- ☐ **155 g (5 oz) caster sugar**
- ☐ **3 teaspoons gelatine dissolved in 1 tablespoon Cointreau and 1 tablespoon lime juice**
- ☐ **1 teaspoon grated lime rind**
- ☐ **250 mL (8 fl oz) thickened cream (double), whipped**

1 Boil, steam or microwave carrots until tender. Drain and place in a food processor or blender and process until smooth. Set aside to cool.

2 Place eggs and sugar in a mixing bowl and beat until thick and creamy – this will take about 10 minutes. Fold in gelatine mixture, peel, cream and carrot puree.

3 Spoon mixture into six individual souffle dishes with a 3 cm (1¹/₄ in) high foil collar attached. Refrigerate until firm. Remove collar and serve.

HONEY AND CARROT RICOTTA ROLL

This carrot roll makes a delightful change from the better known carrot cake.

Serves 8

- ☐ **4 eggs, separated**
- ☐ **125 g (4 oz) caster sugar**
- ☐ **60 g (2 oz) plain flour**
- ☐ **1 teaspoon ground cinnamon**
- ☐ **1 teaspoon ground (grated) nutmeg**
- ☐ **1 teaspoon ground allspice**
- ☐ **1 large carrot, grated**
- ☐ **2 tablespoons golden syrup**
- ☐ **icing sugar**

FILLING
- ☐ **125 g (4 oz) dried apricots, chopped**
- ☐ **125 mL (4 fl oz) brandy**
- ☐ **250 g (8 oz) ricotta or cottage cheese**
- ☐ **125 g (4 oz) unflavoured yogurt**
- ☐ **1 tablespoon honey**
- ☐ **1 teaspoon ground (grated) nutmeg**
- ☐ **2 tablespoons slivered almonds**

1   Place egg yolks and sugar in a bowl and beat until pale and thick. Sift together flour, cinnamon, nutmeg and allspice. Fold flour mixture and carrot through egg yolks. Whisk egg whites until soft peaks form. Gradually add golden syrup and continue to beat until stiff peaks form. Fold through carrot mixture.

2   Spoon batter carefully into a greased and lined 30 x 25 cm (12 x 10 in) Swiss roll pan (tin). Cook at 180°C (350°F/Gas 4) for 15-20 minutes or until firm to touch.

3   When roll is cooked, turn out quickly onto a sheet of baking paper sprinkled with caster sugar, and roll up from the short end like a Swiss roll. Stand until cold.

4   To make filling, soak apricots in brandy for at least 1 hour. Place ricotta cheese, yogurt, honey and nutmeg in the food processor or blender and process until smooth. Drain apricots. Fold apricots and almonds through ricotta mixture.

5   Unroll cake when cold and remove baking paper. Spread cake with filling and roll again. Just prior to serving, sprinkle with sifted icing sugar.

ALMOND AND GINGER TREATS

Serves 4

- ☐ **3 teaspoons gelatine**
- ☐ **185 mL (6 fl oz) water**
- ☐ **125 g (4 oz) sugar**
- ☐ **185 mL (6 fl oz) boiling water**
- ☐ **300 mL (9^1/$_2$ fl oz) milk**
- ☐ **2 drops almond essence**
- ☐ **2 kiwi fruit, peeled and sliced**
- ☐ **60 g (2 oz) glace ginger, finely chopped**
- ☐ **ground (grated) nutmeg**

1   Sprinkle gelatine over cold water and stir in sugar. Pour over boiling water and stir until sugar and gelatine dissolves.

2   Stir in milk and almond essence. Pour mixture into four individual serving dishes. Set aside to cool, then refrigerate until set. To serve, decorate with kiwi fruit and ginger and sprinkle with nutmeg.

Carrot and Lime Souffles, Wheaty Peach and Mango Crumble, Honey and Carrot Ricotta Roll, Almond and Ginger Treats

Plates Incorporated Agencies

SPICY PUMPKIN AND PRUNE SOUFFLE

Serves 4

- ☐ 3¹/₂ tablespoons caster sugar
- ☐ 1 teaspoon vanilla essence
- ☐ 185 mL (6 fl oz) milk
- ☐ 60 g (2 oz) butter
- ☐ 3 tablespoons plain flour
- ☐ 3 eggs, separated
- ☐ 185 g (6 oz) pumpkin, cooked, cooled and mashed
- ☐ 1 teaspoon grated orange rind
- ☐ 1 teaspoon ground mixed spice
- ☐ 100 g (3¹/₂ oz) finely chopped pitted prunes
- ☐ 2 tablespoons orange juice
- ☐ 1 tablespoon Cointreau (optional)
- ☐ 2 egg whites
- ☐ 3 tablespoons caster sugar

1 Place sugar, vanilla and milk in a saucepan. Cook over a medium heat, stirring constantly without boiling, until sugar dissolves. Set aside to cool slightly.
2 Melt butter in a saucepan, remove from heat and stir in flour. Cook over a medium heat for 2 minutes. Gradually blend in milk mixture and cook over a medium heat, stirring constantly, until mixture boils and thickens. Remove from heat and quickly whisk in egg yolks.
3 Combine pumpkin, orange rind, mixed spice, prunes, orange juice and Cointreau and stir into egg yolk mixture. Whisk egg whites until stiff peaks form, then fold through pumpkin mixture. Grease a 20 cm (8 in) souffle dish and a piece of baking paper large enough to wrap around the outside of the souffle dish and extending 3 cm (1¹/₄ in) above dish. Sprinkle dish and paper with caster sugar and secure paper around outside of dish with string.
4 Spoon souffle mixture into prepared souffle dish and bake at 180°C (350°F/Gas 4) for 25-30 minutes or until cooked.

WHOLEMEAL FLAPJACKS WITH HONEY BUTTER

Serves 4

- ☐ 60 g (2 oz) self-raising flour
- ☐ 60 g (2 oz) wholemeal self-raising flour
- ☐ 4 tablespoons powdered milk
- ☐ 2¹/₂ teaspoons baking powder
- ☐ 1 tablespoon brown sugar
- ☐ 1 egg, lightly beaten
- ☐ 250 mL (8 fl oz) water
- ☐ 30 g (1 oz) polyunsaturated margarine, melted

HONEY BUTTER

- ☐ 125 g (4 oz) unsalted butter
- ☐ 1¹/₂ tablespoons honey
- ☐ 1 tablespoon icing sugar
- ☐ 1 teaspoon grated lemon rind

1 To make flapjacks, sift self-raising and wholemeal flours, milk powder, baking powder and sugar into a large mixing bowl. Return husks to the bowl. Stir in egg, water and margarine and beat to a smooth batter using a wooden spoon.
2 Drop approximately 2 tablespoons of batter into a heated, lightly greased frypan and cook until bubbly and browned underneath, then turn and cook other side. Remove from pan and set aside to keep warm. Repeat with remaining mixture.
3 To make Honey Butter, place butter, honey, icing sugar and lemon rind in a bowl and beat until smooth and creamy. Serve with warm flapjacks.

APRICOT PASSION FRUIT SLICE

Serves 6

- ☐ 140 g (4¹/₂ oz) rolled oats
- ☐ 125 g (4 oz) brown sugar
- ☐ 125 g (4 oz) wholemeal self-raising flour
- ☐ 185 g (6 oz) polyunsaturated margarine, melted
- ☐ 2 teaspoons grated lemon rind

FILLING

- ☐ 155 g (5 oz) dried apricots, chopped
- ☐ 125 mL (4 fl oz) water
- ☐ 60 mL (2 fl oz) passion fruit pulp
- ☐ 2 tablespoons raw sugar

1 Place oats, sugar and flour in a large bowl, stir in margarine and lemon rind and mix well. Press half the mixture over the base of a greased 18 x 28 cm (7 x 11 in) shallow cake pan (tin).
2 To make filling, combine apricots, water, passion fruit pulp and sugar in a saucepan. Bring to the boil, then reduce heat and simmer until apricots are soft and all liquid is absorbed. Set aside for 5 minutes to cool slightly. Spread evenly over base.
3 Sprinkle remaining oat mixture over filling and bake at 180°C (350°F/Gas 4) for 45 minutes, or until browned and crisp. Cut into slices and serve warm with cream or yogurt.

Spicy Pumpkin and Prune Souffle, Apricot Passion Fruit Slice, Wholemeal Flapjacks with Honey Butter

Tiles Pazotti Plates The Bay Tree

APPLE WAFER STACKS WITH PECAN SAUCE

Serves 4

- [ ] **1 egg white**
- [ ] **3 tablespoons caster sugar**
- [ ] **$^1/_2$ teaspoon vanilla**
- [ ] **30 g (1 oz) butter, melted**
- [ ] **30 g (1 oz) ground hazelnuts**
- [ ] **3 tablespoons plain flour, sifted**
- [ ] **3 tablespoons icing sugar**

APPLE FILLING
- [ ] **2 large green apples, cored, peeled and sliced thinly**
- [ ] **2 tablespoons honey**
- [ ] **4 tablespoons water**
- [ ] **2 tablespoons sultanas**
- [ ] **1 teaspoon grated lemon rind**

PECAN SAUCE
- [ ] **100 g (3$^1/_2$ oz) caster sugar**
- [ ] **3 tablespoons water**
- [ ] **125 mL (4 fl oz) cream (single)**
- [ ] **45 g (1$^1/_2$ oz) polyunsaturated margarine**
- [ ] **3 tablespoons chopped pecans**

1   Place egg white in a mixing bowl and whisk until soft peaks form. Gradually add sugar, beating well after each addition. Fold in vanilla, butter, nuts and flour.

2   Place heaped teaspoons of mixture on lightly greased oven trays, about 10 cm (4 in) apart. Spread mixture out to about 5 cm (2 in) in diameter, using the back of a spoon. Bake at 180°C (350°F/Gas 4) for 5 minutes or until edges are golden. Cool on trays for 2-3 minutes before lifting on to wire racks to cool completely. Repeat with remaining mixture to make sixteen biscuits.

3   To make filling, place apples, honey and water in a saucepan. Bring to the boil, then reduce heat and simmer covered for 10-15 minutes, or until apples are soft. Stir in sultanas and lemon peel. Set aside.

4   To make sauce, place sugar and water in a saucepan. Cook over a medium heat, stirring constantly, without boiling, until sugar dissolves. Then bring to the boil and boil without stirring until mixture is a light golden colour. Remove pan from heat and carefully stir in cream. Cook over a medium heat, stirring constantly, until mixture is smooth. Stir in margarine and nuts.

5   Place one biscuit on four serving plates, and spread each with apple filling. Top with another biscuit and repeat with remaining filling and biscuits, making a stack of four biscuits, finishing with a biscuit. Dust with icing sugar, spoon over sauce and serve immediately.

> ## MILK
> In the recipes in this book 'milk' has been stated, but you may wish to use unflavoured soya drink. This product is also good for children who have an allergy to the protein in cows' milk, or for people unable to digest lactose (milk sugar). Although it is cholesterol free, it can contain just as much fat as full cream milk and is not as rich in calcium – unless fortified with added calcium. Therefore, it is not always a good substitute.

Apple Wafer Stacks with Pecan Sauce

Glass The Bay Tree

STRAWBERRY AND RHUBARB SOUFFLES

Light, sweet and tangy, these individual souffles will complement a rich main meal. Sprinkled with icing sugar and served with fresh strawberries and whipped cream, who could possibly resist them?

Serves 4

- ☐ **155 g (5 oz) strawberries, halved**
- ☐ **155 g (5 oz) chopped fresh rhubarb**
- ☐ **155 g (5 oz) caster sugar**
- ☐ **2 tablespoons lemon juice**
- ☐ **3 teaspoons gelatine dissolved in 2 tablespoons hot water**
- ☐ **2 egg whites**
- ☐ **250 mL (8 fl oz) thickened cream (double), lightly whipped**

1   Place strawberries, rhubarb, sugar and lemon juice in a saucepan and cook over a medium heat, stirring until sugar dissolves. Bring to the boil, then reduce heat and simmer covered for 15 minutes or until rhubarb is tender. Remove from heat. Push mixture through a sieve into a bowl and stir in gelatine mixture. Set aside to cool.

2   Whisk egg whites until stiff peaks form and fold into strawberry mixture. Fold in cream and spoon mixture into six individual souffle dishes with 3 cm (1¹/4 in) high foil collars attached. Refrigerate until firm. Remove foil collars and serve.

❖

RASPBERRY PASSION FRUIT SORBET

A refreshingly icy dessert that is most suitable to follow a curry, satay or other spicy dish. Fresh, frozen or drained canned raspberries can be used for the puree in this recipe.

Serves

- ☐ **500 mL (16 fl oz) water**
- ☐ **125 g (4 oz) sugar**
- ☐ **60 mL (2 fl oz) sieved passion fruit juice**
- ☐ **125 mL (4 fl oz) sieved raspberry puree**
- ☐ **1 egg white**

1   Combine water and sugar in a saucepan and cook over a low heat, stirring constantly, until sugar dissolves. Bring to the boil, reduce heat and simmer for 2 minutes. Remove from heat and set aside to cool.

2   Stir passion fruit juice and raspberry puree into syrup. Pour into a freezer tray and freeze until firm.

3   Chop mixture roughly and place in a food processor or blender with egg white and process until smooth. Return mixture to freezer tray and freeze until firm.

COOK'S TIP

The sorbet can be beaten using an electric mixer rather than a food processor. Just beat the mixture until it is smooth.

Strawberry and Rhubarb Souffles, Almond Cherry Gateau (page 76), Raspberry Passion Fruit Sorbet

ALMOND CHERRY GATEAU

Creamy-filled and layered, this gateau is magnificent for any special occasion. The gateau is best refrigerated for several hours before serving.

Serves 8

- ☐ **3 eggs**
- ☐ **1 teaspoon almond essence**
- ☐ **60 g (2 oz) caster sugar**
- ☐ **4 tablespoons self-raising flour sifted with 2 tablespoons cornflour**
- ☐ **60 g (2 oz) ground almonds**

CHERRY FILLING
- ☐ **100 g (3¹/₂ oz) cherry conserve**
- ☐ **250 g (8 oz) ricotta cheese**

CREAM TOPPING
- ☐ **3 tablespoons cherry conserve**
- ☐ **185 g (6 oz) cream cheese**
- ☐ **2 tablespoons icing sugar, sifted**
- ☐ **60 mL (2 fl oz) cream (single)**
- ☐ **60 g (2 oz) flaked almonds, toasted**

1 Place eggs, essence and sugar in a mixing bowl and beat until very thick and creamy. This will take about 10 minutes. Fold in flour mixture and almonds. Pour batter into a greased and lined 23 cm (9 in) round cake pan (tin). Bake at 180°C (350°F/ Gas 4) for 20-25 minutes, or until sponge is golden and springs back when gently touched with fingertips. Carefully turn out onto a wire rack to cool. When cold cut into three even layers.

2 To make filling, place cherry conserve and ricotta cheese in a food processor or blender and process until smooth.

3 Place one sponge layer on serving plate and spread with half the filling. Top with another sponge layer and remaining filling. Place remaining sponge layer on top and refrigerate for 10 minutes.

4 To make topping, place cherry conserve, cream cheese and icing sugar in a food processor or blender and process until smooth. Pour in cream and continue to process until smooth and thick. Spread topping over top and sides of gateau. Press flaked almonds around side of gateau and refrigerate until ready to serve.

Carob Hazelnut Macaroons, Rosewater Rice Pudding

ROSEWATER RICE PUDDING

Serves 4

- ☐ **1 litre (1³/₄ pt) milk**
- ☐ **185 g (6 oz) caster sugar**
- ☐ **185 g (6 oz) short-grain rice**
- ☐ **2 egg yolks, lightly beaten**
- ☐ **2 tablespoons rosewater**
- ☐ **ground cardamom**

1 Combine milk and sugar in a heavy-based saucepan, bring to the boil and stir in rice. Reduce heat to lowest possible temperature, cover with tight-fitting lid and cook for 1 hour, or until almost all the milk has been absorbed. Stir occasionally during cooking.

2 Stir in egg yolks and rosewater and remove from heat. Spoon rice into four individual serving dishes or one large dish and dust with cardamom.

CAROB HAZELNUT MACAROONS

Carob and hazelnuts combine to make a deliciously new version of an old favourite.

Makes 30

- ☐ **2 eggs, separated**
- ☐ **185 g (6 oz) caster sugar**
- ☐ **2 tablespoons carob powder, sifted**
- ☐ **250 g (8 oz) desiccated coconut**
- ☐ **60 g (2 oz) roasted hazelnuts, finely chopped**
- ☐ **100 g (3¹/₂ oz) carob, melted**

1 Whisk egg whites until soft peaks form. Add sugar, a spoonful at a time, beating well after each addition, until mixture is of meringue consistency.

2 Beat egg yolks with carob powder and lightly fold through egg white mixture. Stir in coconut and hazelnuts. Drop tablespoons of mixture onto greased oven trays and bake at 180°C (350°F/Gas 4) for 15 minutes or until firm. Cool on trays. Drizzle with carob.

Peach Jelly with Coconut Fraiche

PEACH JELLY WITH COCONUT FRAICHE

This light dessert with a tangy fruit flavour is guaranteed to tempt all!

Serves 6

- ☐ **250 mL (8 fl oz) water**
- ☐ **125 g (4 oz) sugar**
- ☐ **2 tablespoons gelatine dissolved in 125 mL (4 fl oz) hot water**
- ☐ **250 mL (8 fl oz) peach nectar**
- ☐ **155 mL (5 fl oz) strained fresh orange juice**
- ☐ **125 mL (4 fl oz) canned pineapple juice**

COCONUT FRAICHE
- ☐ **250 mL (8 fl oz) thickened cream (double)**
- ☐ **3 tablespoons coconut cream**
- ☐ **1 tablespoon desiccated coconut**
- ☐ **3 tablespoons buttermilk**

1 Combine water and sugar in a saucepan and stir over a medium heat until sugar dissolves. Bring to the boil, then remove from heat and stir in gelatine, peach nectar, orange and pineapple juices.

2 Pour mixture into an oiled decorative 1.2 litre (2 pt) mould, or six individual moulds and refrigerate until firm.

3 To make Coconut Fraiche, combine cream, coconut cream, coconut and buttermilk in a bowl and whisk until smooth. Cover and set aside to stand at room temperature for 24 hours or until mixture is thick. When fraiche has thickened, cover and refrigerate until required.

4 To serve, unmould jelly and accompany with fraiche.

These recipes are like the icing on the cake.
They provide the little extras that make the difference
between a good meal and a memorable one.

GOOD
companions

❖

EGGPLANT (AUBERGINE) CHATNI RELISH

Spread on toast, add grated cheese and grill. Store in a screw-top jar in the refrigerator.

Makes 4 x 250 mL (8 fl oz) jars

- ☐ **2 large eggplants (aubergines), cut into thick strips**
- ☐ **salt**
- ☐ **3 tablespoons vegetable oil**
- ☐ **6 spring onions (shallots), finely chopped**
- ☐ **3 cloves garlic, crushed**
- ☐ **4 small red chillies, seeded and finely chopped**
- ☐ **1 tablespoon finely chopped fresh root ginger**
- ☐ **1 teaspoon black mustard seeds**
- ☐ **1 teaspoon ground cumin**
- ☐ **315 mL (10 fl oz) red wine vinegar**
- ☐ **125 g (4 oz) brown sugar**
- ☐ **1 teaspoon garam marsala**

1   Sprinkle eggplant (aubergine) with salt and set aside for 30 minutes. Rinse under cold running water and pat dry with absorbent kitchen paper.

2   Heat 1 tablespoon oil in a saucepan and cook spring onions (shallots), garlic, chillies, ginger, mustard seeds and cumin for 2-3 minutes. Remove from pan and set aside. Add remaining oil to pan and cook eggplant (aubergine) for 3-5 minutes, or until browned. Remove from pan.

3   Pour vinegar into pan and heat until almost boiling. Return spring onion (shallot) mixture and eggplant (aubergine) to the pan, reduce heat and cook for 2-3 minutes, stirring gently.

4   Stir in sugar and garam marsala. Cook 40-45 minutes longer, or until relish thickens. Pour into hot sterilised jars and seal when cold.

❖

INDIAN PUNJAB SAMBAL

Eat this spicy vegetable relish immediately or store in the refrigerator for a few days.

Makes 4 x 250 mL (8 fl oz) jars

- ☐ **2 red peppers, seeded and chopped**
- ☐ **2 stalks celery, chopped**
- ☐ **2 carrots, peeled and chopped**
- ☐ **2 small zucchini (courgettes), chopped**
- ☐ **2 green chillies, seeded and finely chopped**
- ☐ **4 large tomatoes, peeled, seeded and chopped**
- ☐ **2 tablespoons vegetable oil**
- ☐ **1 teaspoon cumin seeds**
- ☐ **1 teaspoon yellow mustard seeds**
- ☐ **3 curry leaves, crumbled**
- ☐ **1 small eggplant (aubergine), cut into small chunks**
- ☐ **300 mL (9¹/₂ fl oz) vegetable stock**
- ☐ **1 tablespoon finely chopped fresh coriander**
- ☐ **1 tablespoon finely chopped fresh parsley**

1   Place peppers, celery, carrots, zucchini (courgettes) and chillies in a food processor or blender and process until coarsely chopped. Transfer to a bowl and stir in tomatoes.

2   Heat oil in a saucepan and cook cumin, mustard seeds and curry leaves over a high heat for 2-3 minutes. Reduce heat, stir in eggplant (aubergine) and cook for 2 minutes, stirring occasionally.

3   Add vegetable mixture, stock, coriander and parsley. Bring to the boil, reduce heat and simmer for 25-30 minutes, or until liquid has evaporated and vegetables are tender.

Glassware Villeroy & Boch

❖

FIG AND WALNUT CHUTNEY

A splendid accompaniment for your next cheese platter.

Makes 7 x 250 mL (8 fl oz) jars

- ☐ **750 g (1¹/₂ lb) dried figs, cut into quarters**
- ☐ **2 large onions, sliced**
- ☐ **185 g (6 oz) walnuts, roughly chopped**
- ☐ **90 g (3 oz) dried dates, pitted and roughly chopped**
- ☐ **90 g (3 oz) sultanas**
- ☐ **60 g (2 oz) preserved root ginger, chopped**
- ☐ **¹/₂ teaspoon yellow mustard seeds**
- ☐ **¹/₂ teaspoon ground cinnamon**
- ☐ **250 g (8 oz) brown sugar**
- ☐ **750 mL (1¹/₄ pt) brown vinegar**

1 Combine figs, onions, walnuts, dates, sultanas, ginger, mustard seeds, cinnamon, sugar and vinegar in a large saucepan. Cook over a gentle heat for 10 minutes, stirring frequently, or until sugar dissolves.

2 Bring to the boil, then reduce heat and simmer uncovered for 1¹/₂-2 hours, or until chutney is dark and thick. Pour into hot sterilised jars and seal when cold.

❖

MANGO CHILLI SALSA

If fresh mangoes are not available, frozen or canned mangoes can be used instead.

Serves 4

- ☐ **2 large mangoes, peeled and chopped**
- ☐ **2 spring onions (shallots), chopped**
- ☐ **1 small red chilli, seeded and finely chopped**
- ☐ **1 tablespoon finely chopped fresh coriander**
- ☐ **2 tablespoons fresh orange juice**
- ☐ **freshly ground black pepper**

Place mangoes, spring onions (shallots), chilli, coriander and orange juice in a bowl and toss to combine. Season to taste with pepper and set aside to stand for 1 hour before serving.

Clockwise from top left: Coriander Pesto (page 81), Fig and Walnut Chutney, Mango Chilli Salsa, Eggplant (Aubergine) Chatni Relish, Indian Punjab Sambal, Lime and Coriander Chutney (page 81)

LIME AND CORIANDER CHUTNEY

Makes 3 x 250 mL (8 fl oz) jars

- [ ] **10 limes, thinly sliced**
- [ ] **4 large pears, peeled, cored and cut into chunks**
- [ ] **2 cloves garlic, finely chopped**
- [ ] **375 g (12 oz) brown sugar**
- [ ] **4 tablespoons finely chopped fresh coriander**
- [ ] **185 mL (6 fl oz) brown vinegar**
- [ ] **185 mL (6 fl oz) water**
- [ ] **$1/2$ teaspoon ground mixed spice**
- [ ] **$1/2$ teaspoon ground cinnamon**
- [ ] **$1/2$ teaspoon finely chopped preserved root ginger**

1 Place limes, pears, garlic, sugar, coriander, vinegar, water, mixed spice, cinnamon and ginger in a large saucepan.
2 Cook over a low heat, stirring, until sugar dissolves. Bring to the boil, then reduce heat and simmer, stirring frequently, for $1/2$ hours or until thick. Pour into hot sterilised jars and seal when cold.

❖

DRIED APRICOT AND ALMOND CHUTNEY

A sweet, spicy chutney with a nutty crunch!

Makes 5 x 250 mL (8 fl oz) jars

- [ ] **750 g ($1^1/2$ lb) dried apricots**
- [ ] **1 litre ($1^3/4$ pt) hot water**
- [ ] **8 cloves garlic, finely chopped**
- [ ] **315 g (10 oz) sugar**
- [ ] **125 g (4 oz) sultanas**
- [ ] **1 tablespoon finely chopped fresh root ginger**
- [ ] **$1/4$ teaspoon ground cayenne pepper**
- [ ] **300 mL ($9^1/2$ fl oz) cider vinegar**
- [ ] **125 g (4 oz) slivered almonds**

1 Place apricots in a bowl, pour over water and set aside to soak for 4 hours.
2 Place apricots and water, garlic, sugar, sultanas, ginger, cayenne and vinegar in a large saucepan. Stir over a medium heat until sugar dissolves. Bring to the boil, reduce heat and simmer, stirring occasionally, for 45 minutes. Stir in almonds and cook for 45 minutes longer or until chutney thickens. Pour into hot sterilised jars and seal when cold.

Italian Green Sauce with Basil, Mexican Chilli Sauce, Spicy Peanut Satay Sauce, Creamy Mustard Sauce

❖

CORIANDER PESTO

A delicious sauce for pasta, an excellent addition to soup, or just serve it as a dip. It will keep for 2-3 days in the refrigerator.

Makes about 250 mL (8 fl oz)

- [ ] **3 large bunches fresh coriander**
- [ ] **2 cloves garlic, crushed**
- [ ] **60 g (2 oz) pine nuts**
- [ ] **125 mL (4 fl oz) olive oil**
- [ ] **60 g (2 oz) grated Parmesan cheese**

Place coriander leaves, garlic and pine nuts in a food processor or blender and process until finely chopped. With machine running, slowly pour in the oil and process until smooth. Add cheese and process to blend.

❖

ITALIAN GREEN SAUCE WITH BASIL

Wonderful with hot pasta!

Makes 250 mL (8 fl oz)

- [ ] **2 small bunches fresh basil leaves, finely chopped**
- [ ] **3 spring onions (shallots), finely chopped**
- [ ] **2 cloves garlic, crushed**
- [ ] **1 tablespoon capers, drained and rinsed**
- [ ] **155 mL (5 fl oz) olive oil**
- [ ] **1 tablespoon lemon juice**
- [ ] **freshly ground black pepper.**

Place basil, spring onions (shallots), garlic and capers in a food processor or blender and process until smooth. With machine running, slowly pour in oil, then lemon juice, and continue to process until well blended. Season to taste with pepper.

❖

SPICY PEANUT SATAY SAUCE

Makes 375 mL (12 fl oz)

- [ ] **2 tablespoons peanut oil.**
- [ ] **315 g (10 oz) roasted peanuts, finely chopped**
- [ ] **2 cloves garlic, crushed**
- [ ] **1 onion, finely chopped**
- [ ] **$1/2$ teaspoon chilli powder**
- [ ] **1 tablespoon brown sugar**
- [ ] **2 tablespoons soy sauce**
- [ ] **$1/4$ teaspoon five spice powder**
- [ ] **500 mL (16 fl oz) coconut milk**

1 Heat oil in a saucepan and cook peanuts, garlic, onion and chilli powder, stirring for 3-4 minutes.
2 Add sugar, soy sauce and five spice powder, reduce heat and pour in coconut milk. Simmer for 5-10 minutes, stirring occasionally. If sauce becomes too thick, thin with a little milk.

❖

CREAMY MUSTARD SAUCE

Best made just before serving, this superbly tangy sauce is great poured over steamed vegetables.

Makes about 250 mL (8 fl oz)

- [ ] **315 mL (10 fl oz) cream (single)**
- [ ] **$1^1/2$ tablespoons wholegrain mustard**
- [ ] **1 clove garlic, crushed**
- [ ] **3 tablespoons vegetable stock**
- [ ] **1 tablespoon finely snipped fresh chives or finely chopped parsley**
- [ ] **freshly ground black pepper**

Place cream in a small saucepan and bring to the boil. Boil rapidly until reduced by a quarter. Stir in mustard, garlic and vegetable stock. Simmer for 5-10 minutes, stirring frequently, until sauce reduces and thickens a little. Stir in chives or parsley and season to taste with pepper. Serve immediately.

❖

MEXICAN CHILLI SAUCE

Makes about 500 mL (16 fl oz)

- [ ] **2 tablespoons sesame oil**
- [ ] **3 small red chillies, seeded and finely chopped**
- [ ] **3 small green chillies, seeded and finely chopped**
- [ ] **3 cloves garlic, crushed**
- [ ] **2 onions, finely chopped**
- [ ] **1 tablespoon finely chopped fresh coriander**
- [ ] **440 g (14 fl oz) canned peeled tomatoes, undrained and mashed**
- [ ] **1 teaspoon brown sugar**
- [ ] **$1/2$ teaspoon ground cinnamon**
- [ ] **$1/4$ teaspoon ground cloves**
- [ ] **$1/4$ teaspoon ground root ginger**
- [ ] **2 tablespoons lemon juice**
- [ ] **3 tablespoons water**

Heat oil in a frypan and cook red and green chillies, garlic, onions and coriander for 2-3 minutes. Stir in tomatoes, sugar, cinnamon, cloves, ginger, lemon juice and water and simmer for 10-15 minutes or until sauce reduces and thickens.

Learn how to make these basics, and your vegetarian repertoire will be virtually limitless! Your culinary imagination and these recipes can be a dynamic combination.

BASIC
recipes

PIZZA FACTS

❖ Pizzas do not have to be round – some are oval, some are rectangular and some have a deep crust and sides, resembling a pie.

❖ You can make this pizza recipe several days in advance. Let it rise, knock it down, cover with plastic food wrap and refrigerate until required. Bring the dough to room temperature 2-3 hours before shaping and allow it to rise a second time.

❖ Pizzas can be made using plain or wholemeal flour or a mixture of both.

❖ There are two types of yeast that are commonly used in pizza making – fresh and dried.

❖ Dried yeast works just as well as fresh, but takes longer to activate. As it is twice as concentrated as fresh yeast, only half the amount is required. 15 g ($^1/_2$ oz) dried yeast has the same raising power as 30 g (1 oz) fresh yeast.

❖ Fresh yeast will keep in a loosely tied polythene bag in the refrigerator for about a week.

❖ Dried yeast will keep in a cool dark place for about six months. Yeast will deteriorate if exposed to air.

❖ Yeast works best in warm conditions. Cold and draughts slow down its growth, whereas an intense heat will kill it.

❖ The amount of yeast required depends on the richness of the dough.

❖ Fresh yeast works best when mixed with liquid that is at about 25°C (78°F) and dried yeast at 40°C (104°F)

❖ An easy way of making sure that the liquid is the right temperature is to bring one-third of it to the boil and add the rest cold.

❖

BASIC PIZZA DOUGH

Makes a 38-40 cm (15-16 in) pizza

☐ **1$^3/_4$ teaspoons active dry yeast or 15 g ($^1/_2$ oz) fresh yeast, crumbled**
☐ **345 mL (11 fl oz) warm water**
☐ **pinch sugar**
☐ **125 mL (4 fl oz) olive oil**
☐ **500 g (1 lb) plain flour, sifted**
☐ **1$^1/_4$ teaspoons salt**

1   Place yeast, water and sugar in a large mixing bowl and stir to dissolve the sugar. Set aside for 5 minutes or until mixture begins to foam. Stir in the oil, flour and salt. Mix to form a firm dough.

2   Turn out onto a lightly floured surface and knead well until dough is soft and shiny – this will take about 5 minutes. Place dough in a lightly oiled, large bowl. Roll the dough around in the bowl to coat the surface with oil. Cover with plastic food wrap and set aside in a warm, draught-free place for 1$^1/_2$-2 hours or until dough has doubled in volume.

3   Remove dough from bowl and knock down. Knead briefly before rolling out on a floured surface to desired shape. If dough feels too stiff, rest it for a few minutes and start again. Lift dough with rolling pin onto an oiled pizza tray. Finish shaping by hand, forming a slightly raised rim about 5 mm ($^1/_4$ in) in thickness. Top dough with your favourite topping and bake. If a thicker crust is required, cover base with a towel and set aside for 30 minutes or until it has risen sufficiently.

❖

FOCACCIA DOUGH

Focaccia is a large flat oval or rectangle of bread from Italy. In its simplest form it is flavoured with just olive oil, salt and sometimes garlic or herbs.

Makes 1 large focaccia

☐ **1 teaspoon active dry yeast, or 8 g ($^1/_4$ oz) fresh yeast, crumbled**
☐ **30 mL (1 fl oz) warm water**
☐ **300 mL (9$^1/_2$ fl oz) water at room temperature**
☐ **1 tablespoon olive oil**
☐ **500 g (1 lb) plain flour**
☐ **2 teaspoons salt**

1   Place yeast and warm water in a large bowl and stir to combine. Set aside for 8-10 minutes or until it is foaming. Stir in all but 1 tablespoon of additional water and oil.

2   Add one-third of flour and the salt and stir until smooth. Stir in another third of flour and beat well. Add remaining flour and mix until a rough dough forms. Turn out onto a floured surface and knead well for 8-10 minutes or until smooth and shiny.

3   Place dough in a large, lightly oiled bowl, and roll dough around in bowl to coat the surface with oil. Seal with plastic food wrap and set aside in a warm, draught-free position for 1$^1/_2$ hours or until doubled in volume.

4   Knock down dough, knead once or twice and roll to desired shape. Place on an oiled tray, cover with a towel and set aside in the same warm spot for 30 minutes longer.

5   Dimple the entire surface of the dough with fingertips, pushing down about halfway. Re-cover with the towel and set aside for 1$^1/_2$-2 hours or until doubled in size. Focaccia is now ready for topping and baking.

BASIC WHITE SAUCE

Makes 250 mL (8 fl oz)

- ☐ **30 g (1 oz) butter**
- ☐ **2 tablespoons plain flour**
- ☐ **$^1/_4$ teaspoon dry mustard**
- ☐ **250 mL (8 fl oz) milk**

1 Melt butter in a saucepan, stir in flour and mustard. Cook over a medium heat for 1 minute.

2 Remove pan from heat and whisk in milk a little at a time until well blended. Cook over a medium heat, stirring constantly, until sauce boils and thickens.

Variations

Cheese Sauce: When sauce thickens, remove from heat and stir in 60 g (2 oz) grated tasty cheese. Serve immediately, and avoid reheating as cheese becomes tough and stringy if stirred over direct heat.

Mushroom Sauce: Cook 100 g ($3^1/_2$ oz) button mushrooms in butter. Remove from pan and set aside. Continue cooking as for Basic White Sauce, replacing 3 tablespoons of milk with cream. When sauce thickens, return mushrooms to the pan and heat through.

Curry Sauce: Cook 2 teaspoons curry powder and 1 small finely chopped onion in butter. Cook for 2-3 minutes before adding flour, then continue as for Basic White Sauce.

ONION AND HERB YOGURT SAUCE

Try this low-kilojoule (calorie) sauce as an alternative to white sauce. Serve as an accompaniment to vegetables or vegetarian dishes.

Makes 315 mL (10 fl oz)

- ☐ **1 tablespoon olive oil**
- ☐ **1 onion, finely chopped**
- ☐ **$^1/_4$ teaspoon ground coriander**
- ☐ **2 tablespoons plain flour**
- ☐ **125 mL (4 fl oz) low-fat milk**
- ☐ **185 g (6 oz) unflavoured yogurt**
- ☐ **1 tablespoon finely chopped fresh basil**
- ☐ **1 tablespoon finely chopped fresh parsley**
- ☐ **1 tablespoon finely snipped fresh chives**
- ☐ **freshly ground black pepper**

1 Heat oil in a saucepan and cook onion and coriander for 4-5 minutes or until onion softens. Stir in flour and gradually mix in milk. Reduce heat and cook until sauce thickens.

2 Mix in yogurt, basil, parsley and chives and stir over low heat until heated through. Season to taste with pepper.

MICROWAVE IT

Tomato Sauce is made in about 15 minutes in the microwave. In a large microwave-safe jug, cook onion and garlic in oil on HIGH (100%) for 2-3 minutes. Add remaining ingredients. Cook on HIGH (100%) for 10-15 minutes or until sauce reduces and thickens.

RICH TOMATO SAUCE

Makes 375 mL (12 fl oz)

- ☐ **1 tablespoon olive oil**
- ☐ **1 onion, sliced**
- ☐ **1 clove garlic, crushed**
- ☐ **$^1/_2$ green pepper, sliced**
- ☐ **440 g (14 oz) canned tomatoes, undrained and chopped**
- ☐ **125 mL (4 fl oz) dry white wine**
- ☐ **1 teaspoon dried mixed herbs**
- ☐ **freshly ground black pepper**

1 Heat oil in a saucepan and cook onion, garlic and capsicum for 4-5 minutes until onion softens. Stir in tomatoes and wine and simmer for 5 minutes.

2 Add herbs and season to taste with pepper. Simmer for 20 minutes longer or until sauce reduces and thickens.

LIME AND LEMON SAUCE

Makes 500 mL (16 fl oz)

- ☐ **60 g (2 oz) butter**
- ☐ **1 clove garlic, crushed**
- ☐ **$1^1/_2$ tablespoons cornflour blended with 3 tablespoons water**
- ☐ **500 mL (16 fl oz) vegetable stock**
- ☐ **1 tablespoon lemon juice**
- ☐ **1 tablespoon lime juice**
- ☐ **$^1/_2$ teaspoon grated lime rind**
- ☐ **$^1/_2$ teaspoon grated lemon rind**
- ☐ **pinch ground turmeric**

Melt butter in a saucepan and cook garlic for 1 minute. Stir in cornflour mixture, vegetable stock, lemon and lime juices, lime and lemon rinds and turmeric. Cook over a medium heat, stirring constantly until sauce boils and thickens.

❖

RICH SHORTCRUST PASTRY

Rich shortcrust pastry can be used for both sweet and savoury pies.

- ☐ **250 g (8 oz) plain flour, sifted**
- ☐ **185 g (6 oz) butter, chilled and cut into small cubes**
- ☐ **1 egg yolk, lightly beaten**
- ☐ **3-4 tablespoons water, chilled**

1 Place flour into a medium bowl and rub in butter using your fingertips until mixture resembles breadcrumbs.

2 Mix in egg yolk and enough water to form a soft dough with a metal spatula or round-ended knife.

3 Turn onto a lightly floured surface and knead gently until smooth. Cover with plastic food wrap and refrigerate for 30 minutes. Roll out and use as desired.

❖

ALMOND PASTRY CASES

Bake these pastry cases and serve filled with lemon butter or your favourite jam as an afternoon tea treat.

- ☐ **3 tablespoons caster sugar**
- ☐ **vanilla essence**
- ☐ **ingredients for Rich Shortcrust Pastry**
- ☐ **3 tablespoons ground almonds**

1 Add sugar to flour and a few drops of vanilla essence to egg yolk. Continue as directed for shortcrust pastry.

2 Roll out pastry on a lightly floured surface to 3 mm ($^1/_8$ in) thickness. Sprinkle with almonds and cut into 5 cm (2 in) rounds with a pastry cutter.

3 Line patty pans (tins) with pastry rounds, prick bases with a fork and bake at 200°C (400°F/Gas 6) for 15-20 minutes or until golden. Remove from patty pans (tins) and cool on a wire rack.

❖

CHEESE PASTRY

Cheese pastry makes a tasty pastry for savoury pies. Omit the mustard and pepper and this pastry is perfect with apples or pears.

- ☐ **90 g (3 oz) grated tasty cheese**
- ☐ **1$^1/_2$ teaspoons dry mustard**
- ☐ **$^1/_2$ teaspoon cayenne pepper**
- ☐ **ingredients for Rich Shortcrust Pastry**

Place cheese, mustard, cayenne pepper and flour in a large mixing bowl and continue as directed for shortcrust pastry.

BAKING BLIND

✧ Baking blind means to precook the pastry case without a filling. This is done if the filling you are using requires little or no cooking. It is also used when a liquid filling such as a quiche filling is being put into the pastry case. The precooking then prevents the pastry becoming soggy.

✧ To bake blind, line the pastry case with baking paper or foil, then cover the base with uncooked rice, pasta or dried beans. This keeps the base of the pastry case flat during cooking. Keep a container on hand to store blind-bake beans or rice, so that they can be used over and over.

Line pastry case with paper and weigh down with beans, rice or pasta

Tips for perfect pastry making

✧ The best pastry is made using chilled butter and water. It also helps to have utensils cool, so in hot weather it is a good idea to place them in the refrigerator for 10-15 minutes before starting.

✧ Handle the pastry quickly and lightly, as overhandling will result in tough pastry that will be difficult to roll.

✧ The amount of liquid used to bind the ingredients together will vary depending on the quality of the flour. If the dough is too soft the pastry will shrink on cooking.

✧ Kneading the pastry should be done using the coolest part of your hands, the fingertips. After kneading, wrap the pastry in plastic food wrap and refrigerate for 30 minutes before rolling out.

✧ Always roll pastry in light, short strokes, starting from the middle of the pastry, rolling away from you and lifting the rolling pin off the edge of pastry. This ensures even thickness.

✧ Lift and turn the pastry on a floured surface as you roll.

✧ Line the pie dish, trim the edges and rest the pastry in the refrigerator for 10 minutes longer before baking.

Food processor pastry

✧ The food processor is great for making pastry. Place the flour and butter in the food processor and pulse to cut the butter. Add egg yolk and water and process until dough is just formed. Turn out and knead lightly until smooth. Allow to rest before rolling. You may not require as much water, just sufficient so that the ingredients bind together.

Filo pastry

✧ Filo pastry is available from most supermarkets and delicatessens and can be purchased from the freezer or refrigerator sections in your supermarket.

✧ One is equally as good as another. However, once thawed do not refreeze. If you are kilojoule conscious, filo pastry is ideal as the fat content is minimal and very little is required when preparing a dish.

✧ When working with this type of pastry, it is important to keep it covered, as the thin sheets have a tendency to dry and break up. Cover sheets not being used immediately with plastic food wrap, then a damp tea-towel.

Set aside some time each week to plan your family's meals. Drawing up a master grocery list as you go, means you will always have all the ingredients you need to create delicious meals. Use the pantry check list as a handy reminder to make your shopping easier.

VEGETARIAN
pantry check list

STAPLE ITEMS
- ☐ agar agar
- ☐ baking powder
- ☐ bicarbonate of soda
- ☐ bran
- ☐ breadcrumbs, dried
- ☐ brown sugar
- ☐ caster sugar
- ☐ cocoa powder
- ☐ coffee
- ☐ cream of tartar
- ☐ flour, plain, wholemeal, self-raising
- ☐ gelatine
- ☐ granulated sugar
- ☐ icing sugar
- ☐ rolled oats
- ☐ semolina
- ☐ tea
- ☐ yeast

RICE AND PASTA
- ☐ brown rice
- ☐ white rice, long- and short-grain
- ☐ wild rice
- ☐ wholemeal pasta
- ☐ coloured pasta
- ☐ selection pasta shapes
- ☐ instant lasagne sheets
- ☐ Asian noodles

LEGUMES
(store dried legumes in airtight containers)
- ☐ selection canned beans
- ☐ selection dried beans
- ☐ chick peas
- ☐ selection legumes

NUTS, SEEDS, FRUITS
(store nuts and seeds in airtight containers and dried fruit in the refrigerator)
- ☐ almonds
- ☐ peanuts
- ☐ cashew nuts
- ☐ pine nuts
- ☐ sesame seeds
- ☐ sunflower seeds
- ☐ poppy seeds
- ☐ shredded coconut
- ☐ desiccated coconut
- ☐ dried apricots
- ☐ dried figs
- ☐ prunes
- ☐ dried dates
- ☐ raisins

CANNED FOODS
- ☐ asparagus spears
- ☐ baked beans
- ☐ corn kernels
- ☐ evaporated milk
- ☐ coconut milk or cream
- ☐ selection canned fruits
- ☐ spaghetti
- ☐ tomatoes, whole peeled or pureed
- ☐ concentrated tomato paste

OILS, VINEGARS, SAUCES
- ☐ olive oil
- ☐ sesame oil
- ☐ vinegar, white, brown, cider
- ☐ balsamic vinegar
- ☐ rice vinegar
- ☐ selection herb vinegars
- ☐ soy sauce
- ☐ tomato sauce

REFRIGERATOR ITEMS
- ☐ eggs
- ☐ yogurt
- ☐ milk
- ☐ unflavoured soy drink
- ☐ selection cheese
- ☐ margarine
- ☐ mayonnaise
- ☐ olives
- ☐ sun-dried tomatoes
- ☐ tahini

FREEZER FOODS
- ☐ filo pastry
- ☐ puff pastry
- ☐ selection frozen vegetables

RELISHES AND SPREADS
- ☐ chutney
- ☐ golden syrup
- ☐ honey
- ☐ selection jams
- ☐ peanut butter
- ☐ pickles

HERBS AND SPICES
- ☐ allspice, ground
- ☐ basil leaves, dried
- ☐ black pepper, whole
- ☐ black pepper, ground
- ☐ cayenne pepper
- ☐ chilli powder
- ☐ cinnamon, ground
- ☐ coriander, ground
- ☐ cumin, ground
- ☐ curry powder
- ☐ fennel seeds
- ☐ ginger, ground
- ☐ mixed dried herbs
- ☐ mixed spice, ground
- ☐ nutmeg, ground (grated)
- ☐ oregano leaves
- ☐ paprika, ground
- ☐ rosemary leaves
- ☐ sage, ground
- ☐ tarragon leaves
- ☐ thyme, dried

BREADS
- ☐ pitta bread
- ☐ wholegrain bread
- ☐ rye bread
- ☐ selection wholegrain rolls
- ☐ wholemeal fruit bread

You've looked through this book. You've tried – and loved – the recipes. Now, how do you put it all together? This chapter looks at creating a balanced meal and includes tips for successful menu planning.

EASY MENU
planning

Perfect Menu Planning

Plan meals: Set aside some time each week to plan your family's meals for the week ahead. Writing down your menus allows you to quickly see if you are going to serve two very similar meals or dishes close together or use the same ingredients. It is also a good opportunity to check the cooking methods that you are using. Being aware of this when writing your menus, will ensure that you use a variety of cooking methods, and you can be sure to limit the more unhealthy cooking methods such as frying. Menu planning eliminates those anxious moments of what to feed the family in an hour.

Shopping lists: As you plan your week's menus, draw up a master grocery list. Shopping lists ensure that you don't forget vital ingredients and that you buy the correct quantities.

Read recipes: If you are making a recipe for the first time, read it through in advance, as this will alert you to any special preparation requirements such as soaking beans, making stock or marinating. There is nothing more disappointing than planning to cook a dish, and then realising an hour before you wish to eat, that it will take you three hours to prepare because the main ingredient requires soaking or marinating first. You will also be advised of any unfamiliar techniques that can slow down the preparation and cooking time. Reading the recipe through and assembling all your ingredients before you start cooking will save you time.

Using leftovers: It is economical and practical to use leftovers from one meal in the next. Use leftover vegetable or nutloaf as a sandwich filling with chutney or relish. Leftover vegetables are great to add to soups and casseroles. Leftover mashed potato can be made into fritters, croquettes or a topping on a pie. Leftover boiled or steamed potatoes make delicious potato salads. Leftover breads, cakes and scones made wonderful bread and butter pudding.

Balanced meals: The most important function of menu planning is to ensure that you are serving a balanced diet. If each meal is nutritionally balanced, it will help to ensure that you and your family maintain good health.

MENU PLANNING TIPS

Choose a variety of foods for interest, taste and texture.
Choose dishes low in fat, cholesterol and salt.

Time Savers

Salad preparation: Save time by storing salad ingredients and some canned products in the refrigerator. Salads can then be served immediately.

Precook ingredients: Precious time can be saved by keeping precooked rice, pasta or legumes in the refrigerator or freezer. Always cook extra rice, barley, lentils, beans and chick peas.

A bowl of cooked rice can be quickly made into:

- Dolmades *(page 18)*
- Rice Fritters *(page 30)*
- An accompaniment for Indian Egg Curry *(page 31)*
- Brown Rice and Vegetable Pie *(page 48)*
- Rice Terrine *(page 56)*
- Indian Sweet Potato Rice Pie *(page 60)*
- Three-Rice Salad Wrapped in Leaves *(page 66)*

Cooked lentils can be made into:

- Lentil Wontons with Coriander Sauce *(page 18)*
- Spicy Pea Parathas *(page 62)*
- A pate. Simply puree and flavour with garlic and your favourite spices.
- A vegetable soup, to make a substantial meal.

Remember to soak: When legumes are an important part of your diet get into the habit of remembering to soak them the night before.

Cook ahead: Cook more than you require then freeze some so that you have prepared meals on hand. If half the family suddenly doesn't turn up for dinner, freeze the leftovers. Freezing in individual portions is great for those times when only one or two are at home for a meal.

Reduce cooking times: If you are always short of time, a pressure cooker may be the answer. Cooking time for legumes will be reduced considerably. Canned beans will also save time as these only need reheating.

Waste not, want not

✧ Vegetable and fruit trimmings are often thrown away. With a little thought, many of these can be used in a variety of ways such as adding flavour to other dishes. Try some of the following to make the most of all your food.

✧ Beetroot leaves and stalks can be cooked like spinach and served as a vegetable. Alternatively, chop the stalks and use tossed in a salad.

✧ Spinach stalks add a great flavour to stocks and soups. They are also delicious when chopped and stir-fried in butter and garlic and served as a vegetable.

✧ Broccoli stems take a little longer to cook than the heads, but are just as delicious. Chop and serve as a vegetable by themselves, or put on to cook a few minutes before the heads.

✧ Apple cores and fruit skins can be boiled in a saucepan with water, honey and spices, then strained and used as a delicious fruit jelly base. Freeze these trimmings until you have 500 g (1 lb) or more to make this a worthwhile exercise.

✧ Parsley stalks are an essential ingredient in stocks and soups and can be either blended or removed before serving. These can be frozen until required.

✧ Celery leaves are great to use as a garnish or for flavouring. Dry in a cool oven, crumble and store in an airtight container. Use as a flavouring in soups, casseroles or stews when you do not have fresh celery.

DREAMING UP A MENU

FAMILY PICNIC FOR SIX

Roasted Red Pepper Quiches
(page 56)
Rice Terrine
(page 56)
Eggs with Fresh Herb Dressing
(page 56)
Marinated Eggplant (Aubergine) and Tomato Salad
(page 61)
Fresh Fruit

WINTER DINNER FOR FOUR

Curried Lentil and Vegetable Soup
(page 19)
Gingered Vegetables in Bread Baskets
(Make up 1^1/2 recipe quantity)
(page 16)
Crusty Bread
Apricot Passion Fruit Slice
(page 72)

MAKE A MEAL OF A POTATO

Sweet Potato Soup with Ginger and Lime
(page 15)
Potatoes with the Tasty Filling of your choice
(page 20)
Watercress and Goats' Cheese Salad
(page 67)
Lime and Coconut Baked Custard
(page 69)

DINNER IN A HURRY FOR ONE

Blue Cheese and Apple Omelette
(page 29)
Wholemeal roll
Fresh Fruit

BARBECUE FOR SIX

Vegetable Kebabs with Nutty Avocado Sauce
(Make up 1^1/2 recipe quantity)
(page 60)
Herbed Hot Dogs
(page 58)
Marinated Mushroom Salad
(page 58)
Coleslaw
Crunchy Almond Honey Bars
(page 52)

FAMILY DINNER FOR FOUR

Spinach and Tomato Crepe Bake
(page 12)
(Use this quantity for a main meal for four)
Steamed Vegetables of your choice
Italian Green Sauce with Basil
(page 81)
Wholemeal Flapjacks with Honey Butter
(page 72)

SUMMER LUNCH PARTY FOR EIGHT

Savoury Avocados with Pistachios
(Make up 1^1/2 recipe quantity)
(page 14)
Polenta Croquettes with Tomato Sauce
(page 24)
Mixed Lettuce and Fresh Herb Salad
Honey and Carrot Ricotta Roll
(page 71)

The specially developed recipes in this cookbook use many ingredients that may be unfamiliar to newcomers to vegetarian cuisine.

VEGETARIAN
foods explained

Agar agar. Agar agar is an extract of seaweed and is the vegetarian substitute for gelatine. It comes in either small transparent strips of various colours, or powder form. When dissolved in water over a low heat, agar agar blends with water and on cooling sets to a jelly. It is very important that agar agar is completely dissolved before cooking. Stir into boiling water and simmer over a low heat for 5 minutes. It will set in about an hour at room temperature. To set 250 mL (8 fl oz) of liquid you will require 8 g (1/4 oz) agar agar.

Buckwheat. Available as roasted or unroasted grains, it is an excellent substitute for rice.

Buckwheat flour. Made from buckwheat, it is wonderfully light and can be mixed with wheat flour or used on its own. Best known for its use in Russian 'blinis'.

Carob. This cocoa-like powder is the dried, ground seeds of the carob tree. Unlike cocoa powder and chocolate, it is caffeine free. Unfortunately, it is no lower in kilojoules/calories than cocoa powder.

Couscous. Couscous originated in North Africa and is a fine semolina made from wheat. However, variations on the

traditional dish can be found in Sicily, France and even Brazil, where it is cuscuz rather than couscous. It is readily available in packages much the same as rice and is served as an accompaniment to a meal. The name couscous applies both to the uncooked granules and the finished dish.

Fructose. Often called fruit sugar, it is the sugar found in fruit juices, honey and flower nectar. It can be used in place of ordinary sugar and is sometimes recommended by health experts as it is believed to have nutritional benefits.

Malt extract. To make malt extract, the soluble part of the malted grain is extracted and boiled. It is used in homemade beers and wines, hot or cold milky drinks and sometimes in baking.

Miso. A fermented soy bean paste used in the Japanese miso soup. You should be aware that most varieties have added salt.

Natural foods. Foods sold as containing no added preservatives, emulsifiers or artificial ingredients.

Organic foods. Foods grown without pesticides or synthetic chemical fertilisers.

Soya drink. Often called soya milk, it is made from cooked then pureed soy beans. An alternative to cows' milk, it has less calcium than cows' milk. Many commercial varieties are fortified with both calcium and vitamin B12.

Soya grits. Precooked soya beans that have been broken up. Taking only a few minutes to cook, they can be added to stews and casseroles to improve the nutritive value.

Tahini. A sesame seed paste, similar to smooth peanut butter. As emulsifiers are not usually added to tahini, it tends to separate and it is necessary to mix in the oil layer before using.

Tamari. Sometimes called tamari shoyu or Japanese soy sauce. Made only from natural products, soya beans and salt, it contains no MSG (monosodium glutamate), which is often found in Chinese soy sauce.

Tempeh. A mould-fermented soya bean product which looks like tofu. It has a very strong flavour and retains its shape well in cooking. Because of its strong flavour it is not suitable for sweet dishes.

Textured Vegetable Protein. TVP is a meat substitute made from soy bean concentrate. A concentrated source of protein, it is available in a variety of forms: chips, chunks, granules, crumbs, bits, minced, diced and strips. Some varieties are coloured and flavoured. It is useful for stews to boost protein content, or in special recipes where it is used as an ingredient.

Tofu. A curd or cheese made from soy beans. Popular in Chinese and Japanese cuisine, it has a bland flavour and is easily digested. High in protein, tofu is often used for casseroles, stuffings and desserts.

Whole foods. Foods that are grown or raised in the natural way – for example, free-range eggs.

Yeast extracts. These are very nutritious and are mostly used in sandwiches and hot savoury drinks. Yeast extracts can also be used to flavour soups and stews.

GLOSSARY

Arborio rice	The classic risotto rice from Piedmont. If unavailable use any good quality risotto rice.
Baby yellow squash	If unavailable use green or yellow courgettes cut into chunks
Balsamic vinegar	A vinegar from Modena aged in wood to become syrupy and luscious
Beetroot	Regular round beet
Bicarbonate of soda	Baking soda
Bocconcini cheese	Small balls of fresh mozzarella cheese. If unavailable use fresh mozzarella cut into cubes
Breadcrumbs, dried	Use commercially packaged breadcrumbs
Breadcrumbs, fresh	1- or 2-day old bread made into crumbs
Butter lettuce	Round lettuce
Cheese, tasty	A firm good-tasting cheddar cheese
Chilli sauce	A sauce which includes chillies, salt and vinegar
Cornflour	Cornstarch, substitute arrowroot
Coconut cream	Available canned from speciality food shops. Chopped cream coconut, dissolved in boiling water to make a thick cream may be substituted.
Coconut milk	Available canned or as a powder which is reconstituted. Coconut milk may also be made by dissolving 60 g (2 oz) creamed coconut in 155 mL (5 fl oz) boiling water.
Copha	A solid white fat made from coconut oil. If unavailable use a pure vegetable cooking fat
Evaporated skim milk	Use light or partially skimmed evaporated milk
Filo pastry	A very thin ready-rolled pastry used extensively in Eastern Europe and the Middle East. Available in several sizes. The large sheets, approximately 47 x 28 cm ($18^{1}/_2$ x 11 in) are used in this book.
Golden syrup	Honey can be substituted
Mignonette lettuce	Gem lettuce
Muffin pans	Deep tartlet tins
Patty pan	A sheet of tartlets tins
Polyunsaturated oil	A vegetable oil high in polyunsaturated fats, such as corn, soya or sunflower
Reduced fat cream	Coffee cream
Rocket	An old-fashioned salad herb, with a peppery taste, which is enjoying a revival. If unavailable use watercress.
Rockmelon	Cantaloupe melon
Sour cream	Commercially soured cream
Sweet potato	Orange-fleshed, known as red sweet potato
Three bean mix	Canned mixed beans
Wonton wrappers	Very thin sheets of dough available from Chinese delicatessens

USEFUL INFORMATION

In this book, fresh ingredients are given in grams and the nearest equivalent in ounces and pounds so you know how much to buy. A small inexpensive set of kitchen scales is always handy and very easy to use. Other ingredients in our recipes are given in spoons, so you will need a set of measuring spoons (1 tablespoon, 1 teaspoon, $1/2$ teaspoon and $1/4$ teaspoon) and a transparent graduated measuring jug (1 litre or 250 mL) for measuring liquids. Spoon measures are level.

MEASURING UP

Metric Measuring Cups

60 mL	2 fl oz	$1/4$ cup
80 mL	$2^{1}/2$ fl oz	$1/3$ cup
125 mL	4 fl oz	$1/2$ cup
250 mL	8 fl oz	1 cup

Metric Measuring Spoons

$1/4$ teaspoon	1.25 mL
$1/2$ teaspoon	2.5 mL
1 teaspoon	5 mL
1 tablespoon	20 mL

MEASURING LIQUIDS

Metric	Imperial	Cup
30 mL	1 fl oz	
60 mL	2 fl oz	$1/4$ cup
90 mL	3 fl oz	
125 mL	4 fl oz	$1/2$ cup
155 mL	5 fl oz	
170 mL	$5^{1}/2$ fl oz	$2/3$ cup
185 mL	6 fl oz	
220 mL	7 fl oz	
250 mL	8 fl oz	1 cup
500 mL	16 fl oz	2 cups
600 mL	20 fl oz (1 pt)	
750 mL	$1^{1}/4$ pt	
1 litre	$1^{3}/4$ pt	4 cups
1.2 litres	2 pt	
1.5 litres	$2^{1}/2$ pt	
1.8 litres	3 pt	
2 litres	$3^{1}/2$ pt	
2.5 litres	4 pt	

OVEN TEMPERATURES

°C	°F	Gas Mark
120	250	$1/2$
140	275	1
150	300	2
160	325	3
180	350	4
190	375	5
200	400	6
220	425	7
240	475	8
250	500	9

QUICK CONVERTER

Metric	Imperial
5 mm	$1/4$ in
1 cm	$1/2$ in
2 cm	$3/4$ in
2.5 cm	1 in
5 cm	2 in
10 cm	4 in
15 cm	6 in
20 cm	8 in
23 cm	9 in
25 cm	10 in
30 cm	12 in

MEASURING DRY INGREDIENTS

Metric	Imperial
15 g	$1/2$ oz
30 g	1 oz
60 g	2 oz
90 g	3 oz
125 g	4 oz
155 g	5 oz
185 g	6 oz
220 g	7 oz
250 g	8 oz
280 g	9 oz
315 g	10 oz
350 g	11 oz
375 g	12 oz
410 g	13 oz
440 g	14 oz
470 g	15 oz
500 g	16 oz (1 lb)
750 g	1 lb 8 oz
1 kg	2 lb
1.5 kg	3 lb
2 kg	4 lb
2.5 kg	5 lb

INDEX

ACKNOWLEDGEMENTS

The publishers wish to thank the following: Admiral Appliances; Black & Decker (Australasia) Pty Ltd; Blanco Appliances; Knebel Kitchens; Leigh Mardon Pty Ltd; Master Foods of Australia; Meadow Lea Foods; Namco Cookware; Ricegrowers' Co-op Mills Ltd; Sunbeam Corporation Ltd; Tycraft Pty Ltd, distributors of Braun, Australia; White Wings Foods for their assistance during recipe testing.

Penny Cox and Meg Thorley for their help during recipe testing.

Donna Hay for her assistance during photography.